DESIGNING ECCLESIASTICAL
STITCHED TEXTILES

*To the memory of Anna Crossley, a most inspiring
and innovative creator of religious vestments for
cathedrals and churches throughout the world. Born
in Chelsea, she took theology at Oxford and, finally,
she lived and worked in San Francisco.*

BOOKS BY BERYL DEAN

Ecclesiastical Embroidery (Batsford)

Church Needlework (Batsford)

Ideas for Church Embroidery (Batsford)

Creative Appliqué (Studio Vista)

Applikations Broderi (Borgen)

Embroidery in Religion and Ceremonial (Batsford)

Church Embroidery (Mowbray)

Designing Ecclesiastical Stitched Textiles (Search Press)

For information concerning stitched decorations and
construction, consult the following books from the
above list: *Ecclesiastical Embroidery, Church Needlework,*
and *Embroidery in Religion and Ceremonial.*

DESIGNING ECCLESIASTICAL STITCHED TEXTILES

BERYL DEAN
MBE, ARCA, FSD-C

With additional text by Canon Peter Delaney and Pat Russell

BURNS & OATES / SEARCH PRESS

First published in Great Britain 1993
Search Press Limited,
Wellwood, North Farm Road,
Tunbridge Wells, Kent TN2 3DR

Author's acknowledgements

I am tremendously indebted to everyone who went to so
much trouble to send me photographs and slides of their own
and other people's work. I regret that it has been impossible
to include them all. I want to express my very sincere
gratitude to Bill Matthews, who has been endlessly patient
and generous in contacting those who might have had
photographs of Anna Crossley's vestments; regretfully, so
few can be included. This also applies to Joan Chloupek,
who, despite illness, arranged to have examples of Anna's
work from Grace Cathedral, San Francisco, photographed by
Vince Riggio. I am most grateful to him.

Canon Peter Delaney has helped me in many ways. In his
writing he has expressed views which are of immense value
and add greatly to the usefulness of the book. I thank him
most sincerely.

To Anthea Godfrey I owe much gratitude for introducing her
past students, whose contributions are so interesting.

The Reverend Leonard Childs and Judy Barry, both very busy
people, have most kindly given me generous help. There are
so many more, too many to mention, to whom I owe much
gratitude.

And to the Archbishop of Canterbury, for allowing the
frontal shown on page 42 to be included

Acknowledgements and thanks to those who own copyrights
and to the photographers for their excellent work.

Page 28, Joan Chloupek, Oakland, USA; page 47 (top), A.C.
Cooper, London; pages 6, 42, Malcolm Crowthers, London;
page 6, The Dean and Chapter, Winchester; page 51 (bottom),
James Fife, Houston, USA; page 19 (bottom left), 20 (bottom),
66 (top), 67 (top), Ian Freeman, Hertfordshire; page 51 (top),
John Gay, London; page 11, Jarrold Colour Publications,
Norwich; page 18, The Dean and Chapter York, Jim Kershaw;
pages 14, 44, The Dean and Chapter Salisbury; page 77, 79, 81,
Jim Pascoe, Surrey; page 25 (top right), 36 (bottom left), 53 (top
left) Dr Harold Rose; page 40 (top), Southlight Studio,
Dunedin, New Zealand; page 25 (top left), 28, 38 (left), Vince
Riggio, Oakland, USA; page 38 (right), Len Robinson, Mel-
bourne, Australia.

Cover
Top left: detail from 'Adoration' panel, Beryl Dean.
Top right: Purple chasuble, Jacquie S. Binns.
Bottom: Altar cloth, Belinda Scarlett.
Back: 'Head of Christ', Beryl Dean.

Title pages
Page 1: Laudian frontal, Constance Howard .
Page 3: detail of the 'Conical Chasuble', Anna Crossley .
Page 5: Kneeler, Leonard Childs.

ISBN 0 85532 752 9

Colour Separation by P&W Graphics, Singapore

Printed in Spain by Elkar S. Coop. 48012 Bilbao, Spain

CONTENTS

Nave altar cloth for Winchester Cathedral, created by Belinda Scarlett, 1990.

INTRODUCTION

The intention of this book is to show the enormous variety of design, technique and expertise available today in stitched textiles. Modern ecclesiastical vesture is influenced by the same traditional forms that have evolved over the centuries, but these are now adapted to meet new challenges.

The demands of contemporary worship range from traditional Latin Masses to informal Parish Praise. The requirements of such wide expressions of liturgical worship challenge designers and craftsmen alike to offer the very best of their talents for the present cultural climate of the buildings used for worship today.

The question of the brief presented to the designer, however, presents one of the great problems of designing for the Church. For a designer, architect or craftsman to function properly it is essential that they understand the brief of the client, or patron. What part is the commissioned article to play in the life of the church community? What size is it to be; what texture; is it to be largely ornamental or should it have a certain durability to allow for regular use and, not least, what funds are available for the commission? Without a thorough appreciation of the context in which the article is to be used it becomes impossible for design expertise and imagination to be combined in both a practical and a creative way.

It is hoped that the solution to these problems may be arrived at by studying the illustrations in this book. You will be able to see how designers, embroiderers and experts in fabric have attempted to solve the immense problems of providing the Christian community with the best possible interpretation of concepts, in relation to architectural and liturgical demands. This opportunity to absorb a huge variety of stitched textiles may encourage a more careful look at the examples in churches, chapels and cathedrals throughout the country. It may also stimulate a desire to become involved in commissioning designs and, in so doing, you will gain a better understanding of the expertise needed in modern ecclesiastical embroidery. The way a church worships, the building, the colours and the shapes used are all strong indications of its priorities and beliefs.

It is regrettable that of all the excellent altar frontals, vestments, hangings and corporate projects created in embroidered textiles it has only been possible to reproduce comparatively few. It is my hope, however, that they may inspire designers of the future!

An original design for a banner by Beryl Dean.

Aspects of design

All aspects of art for the Church, especially design, are of particular importance at this time of swiftly changing visual concepts. This interesting situation presents the stimulus and the opportunity for introducing good up-to-date ideas, and examples which have been created within the last twenty years can be studied in the following pages. The Church has traditionally been the great patron of the arts and some important developments are taking place. It is hoped that additional familiarity will help those unused to a modern approach to stitched textiles to find a better understanding and appreciation of present-day tendencies in church art, especially when applied to the designing of embroideries.

Most creative ideas have been modern in their time, yet many people find it very difficult to accept this and continue to hark back with longing to the 'traditional' approach. Regrettably, these views are sometimes held by those who are in a position to select, accept or commission work, thereby influencing the choice and, possibly, weakening the impact which a strong contribution from one of today's artists could make to the life of the church. Conversely, there are those cathedrals which have been responsible for commissioning magnificent works, some of which are illustrated in this book, and demonstrate the foresight of the instigators in their contribution to posterity (pp. 6, 14, 16).

It is important that those whose skills are devoted to stitching and making artefacts for a place of worship should really study the examples illustrated here because they are not only well designed but are practical. This collection gives the amateur the opportunity to gain inspiration by precept. Professional designers, and many others who were eager to contribute their skills, have generously allowed their work to be reproduced (pp. 8, 9, 43, 47 (top)). Those who wish to gain experience will benefit from these marvellous examples of contemporary textiles for the Church.

The ability to design is a gift which is instinctive, and so is a sense of colour, but both can be developed. These creative urges, when stimulated and guided, will give expression to forms which, when organized, will produce patterns. In many instances helpful, practical information, and explanations accompany the illustrations; these notes should interest and encourage the less experienced to design.

Canon Peter Delaney writes: 'As a practising artist before entering the Church, I trust that the following observations will be of help and interest to all designers.'

Paraments, created by Tinka Tarva, for St John's Chapel, Bishop Jones Center, San Antonio, Texas. The cope and chasuble are hung on the walls to help worshippers feel surrounded by the light of God's presence. The silk embroidery is combined with quilting, and the colour is air-brushed with dyes.

'God's People on the Way'. A hanging, measuring 1.5 x 2.4m (5 x 8ft), in appliqué and embroidery. Made by the Benedictine Nuns at Turvey Abbey for their own chapel.

Planning a design

One definition of the word 'design' is 'to plan or invent something' and as a definition in connection with designing for the Church it is very apt. In order to plan something you need information, creative ideas, a certain knowledge and inventiveness. These are the foundations of all good design. I can remember being confused as a young art student at the amount of time I had to spend in a foundation course, splitting open apples and oranges, nuts and flowers, and drawing, in detail, that which I discovered about the form and content of these objects. It did not take long before I was fascinated to discover that in the circles and squares, curves and segments, I was beginning to understand the basic structures of creation. To my

astonishment, when I did discover how an orange was made, I also appreciated that the shapes which made up its design were perfectly suited to their function; a network of tiny sacs holding juice, a centre heavily protected with a cavity for the pips, so that they might be cared for until they were needed to produce new fruit from seeds, and so on.

Without this fundamental knowledge it would not have been possible to develop a later understanding of the structure of the human body, its organs and inner workings. Nor would I have so easily understood perspective if I had not learnt to cut through objects and see them in the round. This was an introduction to basic design, and without reaping this knowledge from personal investigation it would have been impossible to begin the critical process of selection and choice. For example, what to retain and what to leave out, or what was essential and what was secondary.

Basic designs and patterns

I eventually embarked on fairly primitive experiments in pattern-making and understanding textures, all drawn from what I saw, touched and felt about life around me. I began to understand how water moved over objects, how light fell and was reflected upwards. I could appreciate that an eyebrow was functional – it stopped sweat going into the eye, the eyelash guarded the pupil from foreign objects – the ear was shaped in its peculiar way to allow sound to enter the ear aperture. This may all seem very obvious to the reader, but to me it was a revelation. I understood what I saw, and when recording the eye, the ear, the eyebrow I realized how they related to the whole design of the head and its functions.

Design and faith

When designers are confronted with translating ideas into signs and symbols, they have to make several important voyages of discovery. First, they must take a journey through their own personal experience, then through the ideas and language about God, and, finally, a journey into a vision and idea of a visual image which attempts to express something of a spiritual nature. I have always found the technical definition of the Christian sacrament a great help in understanding this difficult transition.

'A sacrament', the Church teaches, is 'an outward and visible sign of an inward and spiritual truth'. In other words, through actions, words, ceremonies, signs and symbols, the love of God for man is expressed in human terms, and that means using all the senses in the process. I believe that this sacramental definition can be a help to designers and those who commission designers to work for a household of faith, whether it be a church, a synagogue or a mosque.

Religion uses certain formulae and certain tested symbols to express belief. As the years progress so these beliefs have to be constantly re-expressed in a meaningful and relevant way. Sometimes that means using traditional patterns, sometimes a completely new method and sometimes a combination of both.

Limitations imposed by the Church

All creative designers, whether they work for Church clients or other patrons, undergo certain restraints in their work. These may be imposed because of limited resources, limited space, or limited potential, but they should never be the result of poor communication, or a lack of knowledge or commitment.

The general limitations experienced in designing for the church seem to arise in two particular areas: a poor or badly expressed original brief and a lack of any vision on the part of either the patron or the designer. If these two facets do not work together a commission is doomed from the beginning and there is no hope. Consequently, both of these pitfalls need to be avoided from the start. There must be a clear brief, with a full discussion and the opportunity to produce a variety of attractive designs, before both parties agree on a final solution!

In most cases, a commission from a church community will involve understanding the function behind the design being created. If a vestment is required it is essential to determine its use, its relation to other objects, and who is to use it, and how often. In the case of frontals and hangings, you need to discuss how they are to be hung or draped, how lit, how cleaned and how stored. Above all, what is to be their permanent setting, and how often will they be used?

Inspiration

Most artists and designers depend upon stimulus such as visual inspiration, written description or personal memory to motivate their design, but in the case of a religious subject, as much factual information as possible is a great help. For instance, is there any relevant written biblical material? What is the thematic content of the request? Are there rules laid down about usage or materials and colours to be used for this object or vestment? Where can the designer see evidence of how this had been tackled before? Explore all these avenues before beginning a commission.

The influence of architecture

The visual space which is to be the setting for the new design is crucial to any briefing and discussion about the nature of the proposed design. In almost every case of ecclesiastical design the interior shape, texture and form of the building will be central to the brief. It is important to visit the site more than once, and at different times of the day, to capture something of the nature of the setting. Always ask for information about lighting and the placing of figures in the worship space. Often the architectural forms will inspire part of the design, by dictating colour, pattern and texture. Sometimes a design will need to complement the architectural setting by contrast and a new input. Often a religious building will have an architect who cares for the structure on a regular basis, known as the Inspecting Architect in the Anglican Church, so always try to involve the person in question as a member of the early discussions. If there is a private donor paying for the design, make sure that he or she is consulted along with the Church authorities. The architectural form will dictate scale (below) but as a general rule I believe that most ecclesiastical designs are made on too small and too detailed a scale. You will certainly need to try out your design *in situ* and stand back from it and test its scale.

A religious building is like a theatre or any other public building, where most of the objects fit into large spaces, and relate to each other. The same rule applies to proportions, although sometimes that which is already to be found in the architectural setting conditions the eventual preparation of your design. An arch here, a pillar there, a wall and its colour will help you to decide both scale and proportion.

The question of balance is a much more tricky matter, for so much of the opinions about the balance of a design is dependent upon personal preference. Only the designer can be a real judge of whether the balance of the design works. If you visit the National Gallery in London and seek out the paintings of Botticelli and Raphael, step back and examine the perfect balance of the shapes in the paintings and the careful use of proportion. The weight is always at the base of the picture, one shape leads naturally into another, and if you turn a postcard of one of their paintings sideways, or upside down, they are still balanced and all the proportions work. It is a good exercise to try this out on your own designs.

Nothing is more important to ecclesiastical design and ecclesiastical embroidery than texture. Unlike flat media in paint and line, materials and threads depend upon their texture to work. The movement of different materials, velvet against silk, cotton in relation to leather, laid down thick threads, reflective textures; all of these elements need to be fully understood in order to enable the design to maximise its full potential.

Above all else, at each stage of the making of a new design it is critically important to view the piece being worked from a distance, to see its overall relationship to the whole. In this way all the design elements can be seen as a total concept.

Machine-quilted altar frontal, and set of co-ordinated chevron-striped copes, designed and made by Pat Russell for Norwich Cathedral.

THE USE OF COLOUR

The exciting colours and interesting textures which are obtainable in textiles, threads and dyes are a source of inspiration when creating a work of art for any place of worship (pp. 13, 16).

Considered in relation to ecclesiastical art, the importance of the liturgical colours is significant, but the meaning of the symbolism is not always appreciated by the uninformed designers, nor is the ritual, which has its roots in tradition, fully understood. When properly used, colour helps both the priest and the congregation to feel the mood and true spirit of each different feast or season. 'The practice of defining the church's seasons, feasts and saints' days by the use of special colour only became systematized at a comparatively late date in the Middle Ages. The Lichfield Cathedral's system of Use of c. 1240 is the oldest we now know. Before that, even the great cathedrals were content to use their best and newest sets of vestments for festivals, and the older and shabbier ones for lesser feasts and ferial days. Even after the cathedrals had developed a distinctive system

of Use, it is doubtful if any but the greatest and richest parish churches followed their lead. Abroad, Spain and France developed the most elaborate colour sequences of all and these were followed until the modern Roman sequence displaced them.'

At the time of the Reformation in Britain, during the period to which the Ornaments Rubric, or decorated headings in the Prayer Book, refers, the most general rules, although only very loosely applied, were probably unbleached linen for the first four weeks of Lent and a deep red for the last two weeks, then white from Easter to Whitsun and for the Sundays following. Red was used for apostles, martyrs and evangelists; white for the Madonna and for virgins; blue for Advent and Septuagesima; and a mixture of blue, green or even yellow for confessors. There was no universal ferial colour in England for ordinary services but, generally, a second-best set of any colour would be used for Sundays between the main services, or possibly a green, or a mixture.

Altar frontal, 'The Life of the Virgin', designed and machine-embroidered by Polly Hope for the Lady Chapel, St Peter and St Paul, Borden, Sittingbourne, Kent. The panels are stitched on wool and mounted upon hand-woven silk.

As a guide, the following colours for some of the main festivals in the church calendar are the most widely adopted, although there is no officially prescribed use, except in the diocese of Truro.

White and/or gold: Christmas, Feast of the Epiphany, Easter, Ascension, Rogation days (or blue or violet), Trinity Sunday, Feast of Our Lady, St Michael and all Angels, All Saints' Day, Feasts of all Saints (who are not martyrs), Feasts of Virgins, Weddings.

Red: Whitsuntide or Pentecost, Feasts of the Apostles, Holy Innocents, Feasts of the Martyrs.

This is a bright red, suitable for exultant designs.

Blue or violet: Advent in the Church of England, Lent for the first five weeks (or Lenten white), Vigils.

Purple: Advent, Lent for the first five weeks, Passiontide, Vigils, Holy Innocents, used in the Roman Catholic Church.

Passiontide red: Sixth Sunday in Lent and Good Friday in the Church of England, but altars are left bare. This is a deep, sombre colour, generally trimmed with black orphreys or embroidery.

Green: Epiphany-tide and the season of Trinity to Advent in the Church of England and the Roman Catholic Church.

Black: Funerals, All Souls' Day (or blue or violet), in the Church of England, and Good Friday in the Roman Catholic Church.

Rose pink: After Trinity and as a ferial colour in the Church of England, and third Sunday in Advent. Also fourth Sunday and mid-Lent Sunday in the Roman Catholic Church.

Lenten array: Throughout Lent or first five Sundays only. This is an 'off-white' or unbleached linen, with stencilled or appliquéd designs on frontals, in either red or blue, or sometimes black.

It must still be the practice for most of the poorer parish churches, however, to simplify this use and to adopt a sequence of three frontals only, a best 'white', a ferial of mixed colour, and a Lenten frontal, preferably either an unbleached linen or a blue or violet, if preferred.

We are so familiar with the very basic shades of these colours almost always used that more beautiful variations are sometimes neglected. Conformity to liturgical usage is stressed but, whilst it is adhered to, it is still possible to add interest by selecting, for instance, a green with a touch of blue and grey in it,

or an olive green, which is striking when used with gold. A lighter yellowish-green makes a wonderful foil to a darker green – a touch of green lurex might be added. Think, for example, about pure red as a colour and imagine the wonderful range of mixtures which exists. Refer to the medieval paintings to see its luminous beauty when used in conjunction with dark-greyish, 'inky' blues.

Designers who think spontaneously in terms of colour may find it restricting to have to adhere to the traditional use of the liturgical colours, but the variations are almost limitless. There are still people, however, who take a narrow view; who are unprepared to accept a more liberal symbolism of

Cope, one of a set, designed and embroidered by the late Ione Dorrington for Ripon Cathedral.

The 'Energy Frontal', designed by Jane Lemon and worked by the late Mollie Collins, Catherine Talbot and Jane Lemon, for Salisbury Cathedral. An all-seasons frontal suggesting the primary energies of the physical universe, of nature and human nature, of grace, and of life given and offered. Interpreted as the energy required to be a Christian.

colour; and who can only recognize the conventional and traditional, so depriving themselves of their own spontaneous response to statements in terms of powerful colour. They fail to recognize that symbolism of colour has moved outside the traditional into a wider universal understanding, and is therefore made more powerful because it is not just making an ecclesiastical statement, but also reflects human manifestations. Nobody could remain unmoved by the experience of seeing the 'Energy Frontal' in Salisbury Cathedral (above).

Colour is vitally important to the interior of any place of worship and together with music, it enhances the message conveyed by the spoken word. There is a greater latitude of choice today, and the emotional effect is generally better understood. Chosen with the whole ambient uppermost in the mind, the impact of a brilliant, or alternately, a subtle colour scheme of rich fabrics can be used effectively to contrast with a simple unadorned interior. Vibrant colour and the ever changing pattern of movement have always been closely related to the thrilling displays in nature, which must surely have a relevance to the design of church vestments, making strong human statements which are neither wholly ecclesiastical nor traditional.

The selection of colour is an individual's instinctive expression of emotion, and every artist/craftsman has experienced the thrill of creating glorious colour juxtapositions and undertaking experiments in his or her particular medium. In early times the most precious pigments were reserved for sacred art. Fortunately, today the choice is wide, and a wonderful selection of textiles is obtainable: real and synthetic gold and silver threads and cords; metallic yarns; gold, silver and coloured bullion and wire purls; a wide range of coloured metal threads; leathers, braids, beads, and jewels. Sometimes, however, excessive inclusion can raise

14

a question of taste! The use of dyes and paints extends the possible range of suitable materials in many interesting ways (pp. 23 (bottom right), 42). The planning of colour schemes to be introduced into any place of worship has much in common with working for the theatre, both in the size of the building and the movement and grouping of the participants in the services, or stage productions. It requires experience to envisage the effect of, for example, an altar frontal when it may be viewed from a distance of 60m (65yds); and to plan the scale of the design and adapt the contrasting tonal values of the colours to be used (pp. 6, 11, 14, 16, 47). Small details have been reserved for stoles (pp. 31, 75 (right)). An appreciation of architectural styles and the character of the interior of the building is necessary, together with a real feeling for the ancient stone (p. 11), stained glass, or perhaps, if relevant, uninspiring brickwork.

Before planning any addition to an interior the designer should think about the colours which already exist (p. 59 (top)). It could be a carpet of strident hue or very dominant kneelers. The prevalent colours in the carpet must be taken into consideration, particularly if the design is to be placed in the proximity of the floor covering. An inexperienced amateur is likely to concentrate upon her one object, disregarding all else, instead of seeking the advice of somebody who is trained to see the scene as a whole. These are very real problems which are difficult to solve. A sense of colour needs developing, as does the courage and support to introduce something original (pp. 13, 15). Seldom are there plain white-washed walls which present unlimited freedom of choice.

The fabrics to be used for any commission should be tried out *in situ* in day or artificial light, as the colours and textures can change completely. Sometimes it is almost impossible for the designer to impress sufficiently upon those responsible for the lighting how important it is. Although they have had to make a great effort to raise the funds to pay for the embroidery, those responsible may be unwilling to accept that the lighting is inadequate and, in consequence, the full effect of the work may never be seen.

Of basic importance when planning a colour scheme is the arrangement and grouping of tonal values. To produce the greatest effect, maximum contrast between the tones would be used; that is dark and light (pp. 14, 17) or black and white. Two tones of a similar value next to each other will be lost when viewed from a distance. It is simple to rectify the mistake by darkening or lightening one colour. Because most textiles which are used in a church are seen from a distance, it is important to consider the

Frontal, designed by Jane Lemon and worked by members of the Mothers' Union of the Diocese of St Albans, for the Chapel of Our Lady of the Four Tapers. The theme is purity, with the underlying feeling of fellowship and unity. The design is an abstraction of a rose, a symbol of Our Lady.

tonal values of the colours (pp. 45 (bottom), 47 (top)) and to contrast the size of the area of each, as this will lend emphasis. These simple basic facts can help in the creation of dramatic schemes composed of the interesting fabrics now available.

To examine some of the examples illustrated here will be of help to anyone interested in design. Great importance has been attached to the choice of the textural and tonal value of the fabrics selected when designing the Resurrection cope and mitre (opposite). The density of the black velvet was used to convey original sin; this merged through black suede, oxidized gold and dark grey to a dull cloth of gold and lighter grey which represented life with the hope of salvation through the cross of Calvary; then upwards through the patchwork of light gold and pale grey at the shoulders, leading to the dramatic introduction of white at the tips of the mitre, symbolizing resurrection.

Jane Lemon selected tones of yellow, because it reflects light and the Chapel of Our Lady of the Four Tapers is rather dark (p. 15).

It was important that nothing should detract from conveying the story of 'The Life of the Virgin', so Polly Hope avoided strident colours and a complicated colour scheme (p. 12).

Detail from 'The Flaming Horses' cope, designed and embroidered by Anna Crossley for Bishop Myers, Bishop of California. Full cope is inset.

The 'Resurrection Cope and Mitre', designed and created by Beryl Dean for the Revd Canon Peter Delaney. The progress through life is symbolized by the gradation from the denseness of the black at the base of the cope, representing original sin, through the neutral greys, to the Cross of Calvary and upwards to the everlasting light.

Signs and symbols

From earliest times symbols and signs have formed an integral part of religious art, and were of particular importance when advantage had to be taken of every opportunity to convey 'The Message' pictorially, or through decoration, for example, by means of stitchery. Symbols were recognized and their meaning understood at a time when the laity were mostly unlettered, but this does not apply today. So when critics lament the loss of some traditional symbolism, this simply means that they fail to recognize the contemporary approach and are not prepared to accept an alternative statement.

Relative to the questioning of fundamental ideas concerning the visual arts, Michael Day writes, 'Artists began to see painting on a sculpture not as a representation of something else but as a design in itself', and, 'The new ways of looking at art were a long way from the idea of seeing a work of art as a symbol of the reality of God, and when English churchmen were confronted with examples of modern works it appeared that very few of them understood anything at all about the fundamental new ideas'. In recognizing that a religious work can be created in almost any medium, an idea carried out with threads and fabric can certainly have a deeper meaning and would incorporate symbolism.

The message conveyed by a work of art for the church is directed outside the material to God, and is intended to take the mind and imagination beyond the visual image. It aspires to inspire worship and to deepen awareness through symbols, which are visual and not verbal, and point to the nature of God. This visual art possesses its own integrity, yet is something beyond itself, and communicates a deeper meaning.

Abstract art is expressed through shapes. The vast symbolic imagery can inspire designers to create powerful works of significance and mystery

Lenten frontal, vestments, burse, veil, Zouche Chapel, York Minster. Designed by Joan Freeman and embroidered by York Minster Broderers. The cross and emblems of The Passion are superimposed upon angular rock shapes symbolizing the Hill of Golgotha. Appliqué, laid cords of hand-spun undyed sheep's wool and silks.

Hood and orphrey from one of a set of copes, designed and machine-embroidered by Judy Barry and Beryl Patten, for Chester Cathedral. Design based upon the symbolic use of pomegranates.

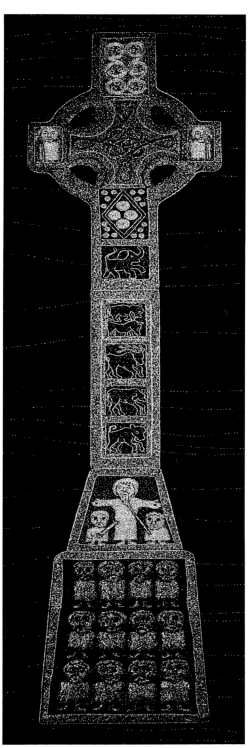

Banner, designed and embroidered in goldwork by Hazel Voakes. The inspiration came from Celtic crosses studied on an archaeological summer school in Eire.

Central motif of the altar frontal, for The College of Corpus Christi and the Blessed Virgin Mary, Cambridge. Designed by Joan Freeman and embroidered by Clarissa Robinson in silk threads and laid gold. The 'Pelican in her Piety', a medieval symbol of the redemptive sacrifice of Christ.

Laudian frontal, designed and embroidered with tubular braids and gold threads by Constance Howard, for the St Mary Magdalene Chapel, Lincoln Cathedral.

Trinity nave altar frontal, designed by Joan Freeman and embroidered by Clarissa Robinson for St Albans Abbey. The Phoenix motif of the Resurrection of Christ is superimposed on three abstract shapes symbolizing The Trinity. Appliqué, silks, laid gold.

which make a strong statement when treated in an abstract way (below). In contrast, and still being produced because of their popularity, are insignificant repetitions of outworn symbols which are no longer relevant. They are interpreted traditionally and lack originality; therefore they fail to make any impact, due to their predictability. For example, the cross has lost much of its sanctity as a symbol by being over-used, almost as a commercial sign. It goes back to the aspect of death rather than concentrating with a wider vision to the Resurrection. There would be complete stagnation in the visual arts unless each age made its own contribution. In this context, symbols interact on a deeper level whereas signs are but a form of notice giving information.

Some critics, familiar with Victorian floral symbolism, may be unfamiliar with, and therefore unsympathetic to contemporary design and colour, so are unprepared to accept anything but the traditional and hark back to the safety of the conventional. Reviewing an exhibition of outstanding examples of more recent ecclesiastical embroidery a critic wrote (to quote but a few short extracts from much more in the same vein), 'Perhaps the most unnerving feature of the exhibition is how unconcerned modern embroideresses are with the traditional symbols . . . only the odd phoenix . . . and angels and saints hardly get a look in. Almost the whole bestiary of sacred animals appear to be extinct and traditional plants and flowers have also largely gone . . . This critic simply could not appreciate or understand any of the colours or the modern approach to symbolism.

Symbolism is used as a gesture of Christian faith, and is meaningful. Although this may not be at once perceived, it is still the basis of design for church embroidery and is its main inspiration as a means of communicating at a deeper level. The problem of how to put across the message of the Church and the way symbolism can open up awareness to another world has been solved in many different ways (pp. 9, 14, 20, 21, 22, 37 (bottom left and right), 53 (top right)).

Shapes represented as having departed from the natural outlines of the objects they stood for are referred to as 'abstract', and can be seen to have a relationship with the concept of symbolism. Colour, too, has important meanings and has had a strong cultural basis from very early times.

The fish, symbol of Christ, designed by Amanda Wright, and based upon a twelfth-century mosaic in a church on the Isle of Torcello. As she made the embroidery, it represented to her the resurrection of the sea's dead and the giving back of life.

21

Designing liturgical vestments

Traditionally, when vesting for Mass the celebrant wears the amice, alb, girdle, stole, and lastly, the chasuble. The maniple is no longer used, and the dalmatic and tunicle are worn by the deacon and sub-deacon respectively. The same fabric is used for the set as a whole and this includes orphreys and apparels, when applicable. It should be of a weight and texture which will hang well, and the decoration throughout should be similar. Most churches would obviously prefer to possess a set of vestments in each of the liturgical colours, although this is not essential. It is important to select colours which accord well with the vestments and soft furnishings already in the church.

Although traditional vestments are still usually worn, in recent years in the quest for egalitarianism there has been a tendency to dispense with some sacred garments, or the need for those officiating to be similarly vested. However, the celebrant or president's chasuble (if used) may be more distinctive. The surplice and cotta may frequently be decorated with drawn-thread borders.

There are changes consequent upon con-celebration of the Eucharist because of the many participants. The Vatican Council and National Synod have advocated that the basic vestment, chasuble or cassock alb, should remain the same: white or stone-coloured linen, or similar fabric, with a detachable orphrey or wide stole, of a colour changing with the season. There may be a central chasuble of a matching colour. The bishop would wear a chasuble and mitre and most Anglicans would wear chasubles.

The design of a vestment must be appropriate and should be a work of art having value and dignity in its own right, and this largely depends upon the suitability of the textiles used. It can be a thing of beauty which is complete in itself, without

Altar cloth and chasuble. 'In the beginning is my end . . . In my end is my beginning.' East Coker *by T. S. Eliot. They were designed by Belinda Scarlett for St Martin's Church, Canterbury, which has been in continuous use since A.D. 562.*

the addition of applied decorations, but it must also serve its function.

Although vestments have been simplified, they are still important. To quote from 'Environment and Art in Catholic Worship', the following remarks are apposite: 'The wearing of ritual vestments by those charged with leadership in a ritual action is an appropriate symbol of their service, as well as a helpful aesthetic component of the rite. That service is a function which demands attention from the assembly, and which operates in the focal area of the assembly's liturgical action. The colour and form of the vestments and their difference from everyday clothing invite an appropriate attention, and are part of the ritual experience essential to the festive character of a liturgical celebration.' In addition to this, the shape and function of a vestment determines its design. If a garment is badly designed it will not fit or hang properly on the wearer and added decoration will not solve the problem.

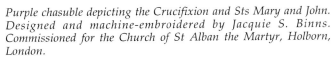

Chasuble designed and made by Pat Iles. Various shot fabrics, some transparent, were machined together with gold machine thread.

Purple chasuble depicting the Crucifixion and Sts Mary and John. Designed and machine-embroidered by Jacquie S. Binns. Commissioned for the Church of St Alban the Martyr, Holborn, London.

Easter chasuble (reversible) painted, oil on muslin, and quilted. Created in 1979 by Tinka Tarva, Texas.

The Chasuble

The liturgical costume of today is derived from the dress of the Roman citizen during the first ages of the Christian church. It was then that the paenula, a woollen outer garment, was eventually replaced with the chasuble, alb and other garments now associated with the Christian liturgy and acquired a special ecclesiastical significance.

The chasuble was originally semi-circular in shape, the straight edges being joined together down the centre front, leaving an opening for the neck. The join was later covered with a strip of material, and this became the decorated orphrey. Known as the conical chasuble (p. 25 and Fig. 1), it is made from soft fabric of the right weight, to fall in deep, rich, horizontal folds. However, this shape was found to be inconvenient in wear, so the sides were gradually cut away, which led to its subsequent deterioration.

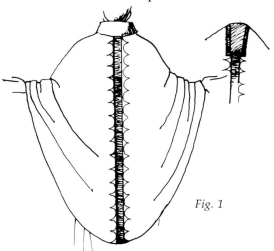

Fig. 1

The so-called 'Gothic revival' chasuble, introduced in the late nineteenth century, was a skimpy garment. The shaping was achieved by having shoulder seams (Fig. 2). The main decoration

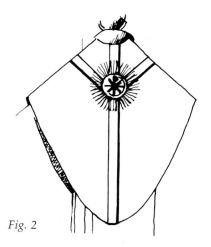

Fig. 2

was upon the back, but these characteristics have now been superseded by the longer, fuller vestment of today. The decorative stitchery can take several alternative forms, for example, the adaptation of the traditional Y-shaped orphrey (Fig. 3).

Fig. 3

The dignified chasuble of today is about 1.2m (4ft) long and about 1.5m (5ft) wide. The total length may extend to within a few centimetres (inches) of the floor at the back, slightly more in front, and the shoulder seams would end at the wrist or beyond. Frequently a collar (Fig. 4), replaces the plain neckline, instead of

Fig. 4

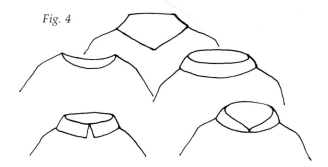

the amice and embroidered apparel. When cut from a wide textile, central seams are unnecessary. In its present-day form the chasuble is interesting to design; however, not only do the colours and character of the existing decorative objects have to be considered when contemplating the design of the vestment, but also the wishes and comfort of the wearer.

There are few limitations to the placing of the ornamentation, the front and the back now being of

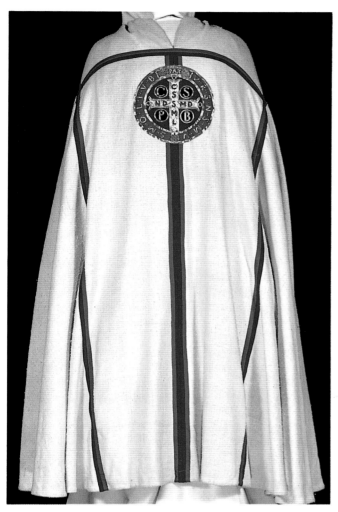

The Conical chasuble, created by Anna Crossley for the ordination of Revd Jack Schanhaar in 1982. Embroidered with the medal of Saint Benedict surrounded with the letters of the prayer and motto.

Red chasuble, designed and embroidered by Katarin Privett, for St Michael's, East Coker, Somerset. A fifth-century Ostro-Gothic cloak brooch inspired the idea. Net overlays the cloth of gold which is stitched with metal threads.

Detail from a chasuble for a woman designed by Conni Eggers, USA.

Three chasubles, in a set of four, designed and worked by Lee Porzio and Mychl Ditson for St Barnabas-on-the-desert, in Paradise Valley, Arizona. The predominant materials are Thai and Italian silks, and the major work is in blind appliqué with details in machine-embroidery. From left to right:

The green, representative of Spring and hope, carries a composite symbol of a harp and fleur-de-lys and bulrushes – 'we are bent, not broken . . .'

The red, both in colour and negative patterns, symbolizes fire, martyrdom and Pentecost. The positive blue suggests wings and soaring of the spirit.

The purple, usually associated with mourning, carries the thistle symbol of Passion.

Chasuble, designed and carried out by Anna Crossley in appliqué for the Revd Wallace E. Spraque, St Luke's Episcopal Church, Calistoga, California.

equal importance. Having decided on the shape of the chasuble, determine where the emphasis of the stitched decoration needs to be placed. There are several alternatives as these can be quite varied and original.

For practical reasons the straight central orphrey, or band of decoration, is most frequently used (p. 23 (top right) and Fig. 5a), or the wider, shaped panel designed for Epiphany (p. 23 (left) and Fig. 5b).

Fig. 5a

Fig. 5b

Fig. 5c

Other alternatives are decorative motifs (p. 28 and Fig. 5c), or the interest can be focused on the hem or neckline (p. 23 (bottom right) and Figs. 6a and 6b). The all-over abstract design is generally chosen when the effect depends upon, say, beautiful Thai or Chinese silks (p. 26 (bottom) and Figs. 6d and 6e). Occasionally a cowl hood may be the focus of interest. A wide band of embroidery around the shoulders is always effective, or an adaptation of the cross (pp. 22 and 25 (top right) and Fig. 6c).

The contemporary designer should consider fitness of purpose to be of prime importance, and the chasuble also needs to be rethought in view of the changes in services which are taking place. The presiding president or priest now faces the congregation, although there is no time when his back is not seen. Another reason for the change is that the chasuble becomes the frame for the elements of

bread and wine, and as such it has to be considerably fuller and longer. This last feature is important, due to the fact that many altars are in the form of a table and are without a frontal, so that the whole length of the garment worn by the priest is seen.

The time will come when not one chasuble, but a chasuble for each participating priest taking part in a concelebration, will be needed, instead of the dalmatic, tunicle and stole worn for a traditional High Mass. These chasubles would conform to the liturgical colour for the season, or a ferial colour could be used.

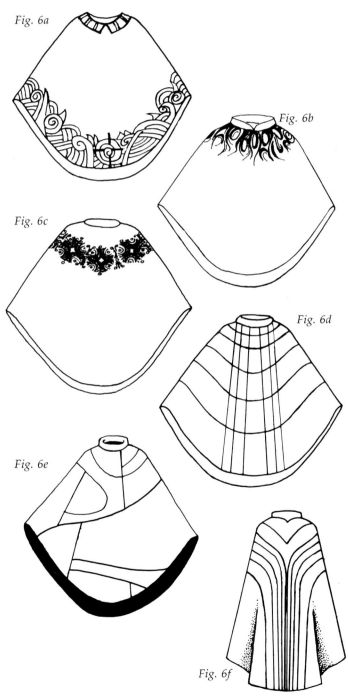

Fig. 6a

Fig. 6b

Fig. 6c

Fig. 6d

Fig. 6e

Fig. 6f

'The New Jerusalem Chasuble', designed and embroidered by Anna Crossley for the Church of the Advent of Christ the King, San Francisco.

The detail below shows the new city, 'with a glad and moving star in its midst', and illustrates Anna's mastery of the technique of goldwork.

Stole

The stole is a sign of priestly dignity and power and it symbolizes the yoke of Christ. Being a part of the set of ecclesiastical vestments, it conforms to the liturgical colour for the season and is generally made from the same material.

Traditionally it is fairly narrow and long, and a repeating pattern stitched along the whole length is always effective (p. 31 and Fig. 7a), or the decoration can be positioned towards the ends. This gives an opportunity for detailed embroidery, as in the technique seen at Fig. 7b. Conventionally, there are three crosses, one at either end and one at the centre back, but this is not obligatory, although the one at the centre back is usual, and in the Roman rite it is essential. The new wide stole (right, p. 30 (bottom) and Figs. 8a, 8b and 8c), is advocated by the Church Commission and it is worn by those taking part in the concelebration. It measures up to 20cm (8in) in width and in length may fall to within 20cm (8in) of the ground, and generally has a shaped neckline.

There is unlimited scope for embroidery, which is usually concentrated at chest level (right and Figs. 8a and 8b), but can be in any position. This stole is normally worn over the cassock alb.

Red stole, designed and carried out by Anna Crossley using appliqué, for the ordination of the Revd John Gardiner at the Church of the Good Shepherd, St Ignace, Michigan.

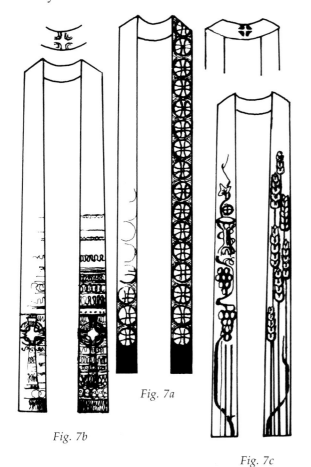

Fig. 7b

Fig. 7a

Fig. 7c

Fig. 8a

Fig. 8b

Fig. 8c

For more simple celebrations of the Eucharist a wide stole is used by each priest who would be wearing the cassock alb. Sometimes this stole is made to be reversible. The Eucharistic stole can be longer than either the pastoral or preaching stole.

The baptismal stole is white, the reverse side being purple. The white side is used for communion for the sick and the purple for confession. The scarf or preaching stole is usually black, or sometimes dark blue, (see below).

Preaching scarf, designed and embroidered in laid and couched goldwork by Arja Salminen, London College of Fashion.

A detail from the ordination stole, for the Revd Jonathon Greener, that was designed and machine-embroidered on wool by Polly Hope.

Set of four wide stoles, designed and embroidered by Anna Crossley, for St John's United Church of Christ, San Francisco.

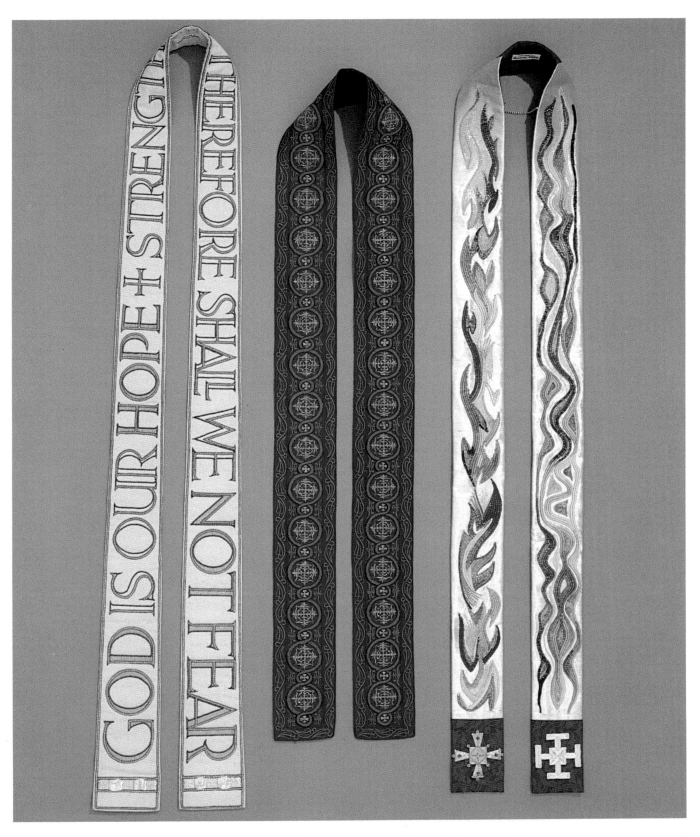

A set of three stoles. Left: The Holy Spirit stole for the Archbishop of Canterbury, 1992, by Leonard Childs. Gold threads couched with silks. Centre: The Holy Spirit stole for F. Dennis King, Chesterfield. Machine-embroidered in 1987 by Simon Nelson. Right: The Chester stole for Michael Baughan, Bishop of Chester. Executed by Leonard Childs in 1983 – hand-couched gilt cords and appliqué.

Dalmatic and tunicle

Usually each church possessed a set of Mass vestments in each of the liturgical colours, including the dalmatic and tunicle. The shape of both of these garments was similar, but the sleeves of the former were considerably wider and longer and could have cuffs (Figs. 9a and 9b).

Fig. 9a

Fig. 9b

Fig. 9c

Today, the decoration or cut of both vestments still suggests the clavi, which were originally two vertical stripes running from shoulder to hem (Fig. 9a). Quite often inverted pleats replace the clavi or bands of hand or machine-stitched decoration (Fig. 9b). The dalmatic had, in addition, two horizontal apparels or orphreys, one at chest level and the other lower down, both back and

front. The tunicle had only the upper apparels, back and front. Latterly these vestments have become much longer and fuller, though still simple in shape (Fig. 9c).

There should be accompanying stoles, the one for the deacon being straight, without shaping at the neck and rather wider. It has an inconspicuous fastening and is worn over the left shoulder.

With the current changes only the chasuble and stoles are required instead of the complete set of Mass vestments.

Orphreys or apparels

The cassock alb has made the amice unnecessary, but should it be required the detachable apparel measures about 8 x 56cm (3 x 22in) and is embroidered. The alb is not always worn now, but if it is, the apparels may be embroidered, the fabric matching the set. Alternatively, the hem and sleeves can be embroidered directly on to the linen, or linen substitute.

Five copes for the Provost and Canons of the Cathedral of Sts Peter and Paul, Sheffield, designed by Leonard Childs and embroidered by him, Pauline Morrison, Jean Leeds and Simon Nelson.

Cope

The cope probably derived from the open-fronted paenula, which was fastened with a morse or clasp. The hood, usually considered an invariable part of the ceremonial cope, was not treated as such, even in the Middle Ages. In the debased baroque semi-circular form the hood descended from below the stiff orphrey, which could be as much as 20cm (8in) wide. The cope is not, strictly, part of the set of Eucharistic vestments.

'There is now a growing tendency amongst Anglicans and Roman Catholics alike to return to the more graceful and ample forms of vesture, based on primitive and early mediaeval precedent', to quote C.E. Pocknee, who pointed out that this earlier shape of cope was lost at the Renaissance; it had had a curved neckline, and the orphrey, which was usually as narrow as 7cm (3in), was also shaped and to this the cowl hood was attached (Fig. 10a).

The revival of the more gracious cope creates a precept for the shaped garment which is worn increasingly today, not only because it is more comfortable in wear, as the cut gives additional fullness, but also because the deep folds add to its

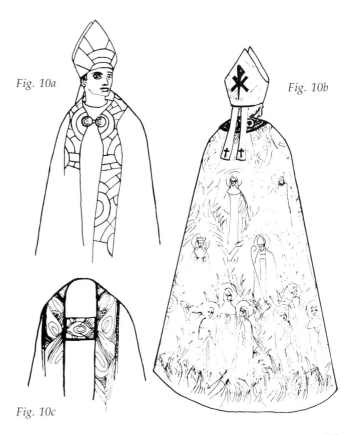

Fig. 10a

Fig. 10b

Fig. 10c

33

dignity. For this shape of cope there can be particular emphasis upon the designs for the embroidery on the hood and orphrey, if there is one.

In its simplest form the basic shape is semi-circular, with a radius minimum of 1.52m (60in), the straight edge of which is taken 10cm (4in) lower than the centre. Because it is not very comfortable to wear, this shape is now seldom made. Slight shaping adds to the comfort and for this the front edges remain straight up to the position of the morse, then they curve outwards about 6cm (2½in), finally curving inwards for the neckline. Frequently there is a fairly narrow similarly shaped orphrey (Fig. 10a). This cope hangs well, and it is possible to work on an all-over design, as there may be no seams (Fig. 10b), or the interest may be centred upon the orphrey and hood (Figs. 10a and 11a, 11b and 11c).

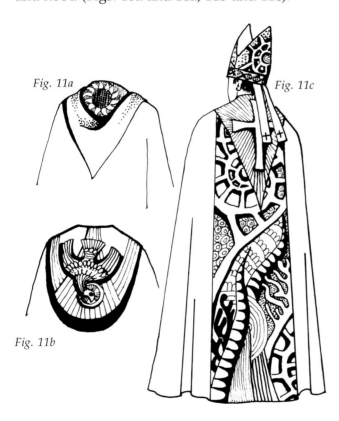

Fig. 11a

Fig. 11c

Fig. 11b

A more ample cope is constructed by joining radiating sections, so forming more than a semi-circle. There may or may not be an orphrey, although there is generally a hood. Variously coloured segments can be joined together to make an interesting colour scheme, or the width of the sections can be adapted according to the planning of the decoration. The hood can be flat or cowl-shaped.

Another form of cope, with shoulder shaping, requires some knowledge of pattern drafting and is more difficult to construct, but this is justified by improved comfort and the way in which it eventually hangs. Wide back and centre front panels are cut, then side back and side fronts are cut with shoulder shaping. Finally, the side front and side back seams are joined from neck to hem (p. 17 and Fig. 11c).

The purpose of any vestment will affect its design and the 'Resurrection' cope (p. 17) is an example of designing in terms of the three-dimensional. Each individual piece is part of, and relates to, the shape of the garment and the fabrics, yet is an integral part of the design as a whole. As it is carried out mainly in patchwork, each sub-division forms a part of a larger shape in the overall design. When it is eventually joined together it becomes a fitted cope, which having been planned in the round relates perfectly to the human figure.

A cope which has been cut and made up as a full circle hangs beautifully (p. 38 (right)). This example was created by Nigel Wright and the design of the symbolism on the hood is of particular interest.

It is not essential to have a hood, whether a cowl (Figs. 11a and 11b), flat, rounded, or pointed (p. 36 (bottom right) and Fig. 10b).

The fastening of a cope is either a metal clasp or a morse, which is an embroidered strip of stiffened fabric (Fig. 10c), with large hooks and eyes sewn on the back. Strips of Velcro, a touch-and-hold fabric fastener, are also a satisfactory alternative.

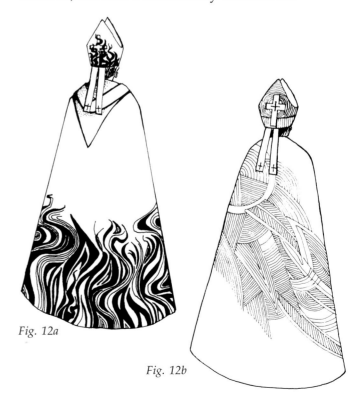

Fig. 12a

Fig. 12b

The semi-circular cope, because it can be treated as a flat surface, without seams, makes designing and working much more straightforward, as the ultimate visual impact can be foreseen. The wonderful medieval vestments demonstrate how a design was planned and soundly structured, instead of relying on ornamentation being applied to a shape. However, it is now usual to achieve the shaping with the minimum of seaming, because the interest in planning a cope is to create a striking design. The design may be all-over (Fig. 10b), or the decoration can enrich the lower edge of the cope (Fig. 12a). As an alternative, the direction of the ornamentation may be diagonal (Fig. 12b). This latter example could be very effective if carried out in couched gold thread, cord, or thick thread. There are endless possibilities for ingenious variations of decoration and experimental techniques, both by hand or by machine.

It is interesting, and something of a challenge, to create vestments for women (pp. 36 (top) and 40 (top)), but it is to be hoped that the sanctity of the garment rather than the feminine aspect will be stressed.

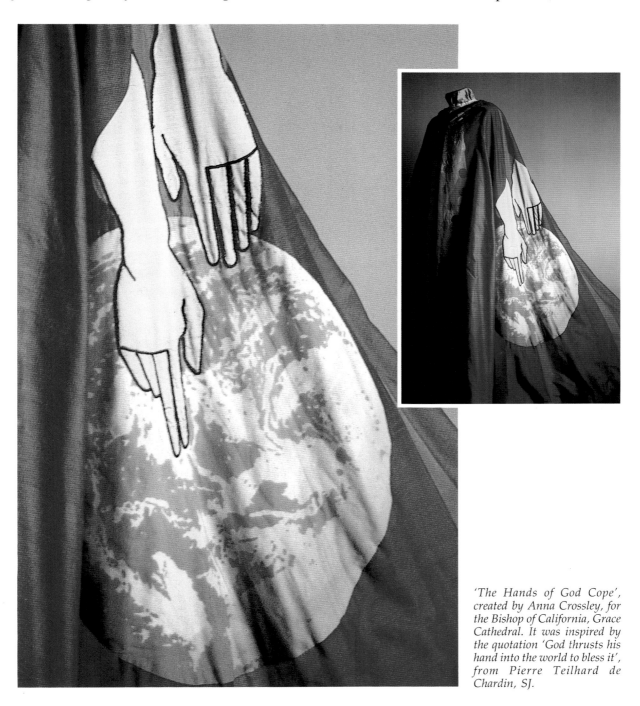

'The Hands of God Cope', created by Anna Crossley, for the Bishop of California, Grace Cathedral. It was inspired by the quotation 'God thrusts his hand into the world to bless it', from Pierre Teilhard de Chardin, SJ.

35

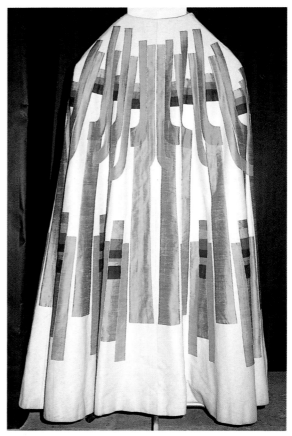

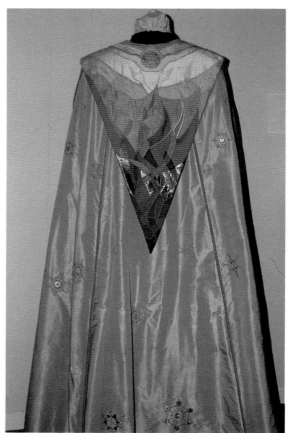

Opposite, top left: Cope for Durham Cathedral, one of a set of seven. The design, by Renate Melinsky, is based upon architectural features and is machine-embroidered.

Opposite, top right: Cope, 'God upon earth rising to glory', designed and worked by the late Ione Dorrington. Created for St Peter-le-Poer Church, Friern Barnet, London.

Opposite, bottom left: Gold cope, designed by Sylvia Green, and assisted by Pamela Benson, for St Michael's, Highgate, London. Embroidered with Japanese gold and silk threads, basket stitch, laidwork and appliqué.

Opposite, bottom right: The Benedicite Cope, designed and embroidered by Renate Melinsky. The fabric is gold silk, for the glory of God and celebration; the blue lining and seam piping is for the rivers, seas and sky; and the snowflakes cascading, none repeating, for the infinite variety of God's creation.

Right: Trinity Cope, designed and made by Renate Melinsky for a woman deacon – briefing, simplicity.

Below left: Cope, designed and worked by Edith Sutcliffe for St Philip's Cathedral, Birmingham. The design is based upon intertwined branches of the Cedars of Lebanon, an ancient symbol of Christ. The background is heavy pure silk with applied silks and other fabrics. Machine- and hand-embroidery, and goldwork methods. The morse is by Frank Sutcliffe.

Below right: Cope, 'The Tree of Life', designed by Marjory Morton and embroidered by her and Elizabeth Carpenter, for Eton College Chapel. The tree is depicted growing from earth, rocks and minerals surrounded by sea and light from the Eye of God. The method of overlaying organzas was inspired by Chinese painting.

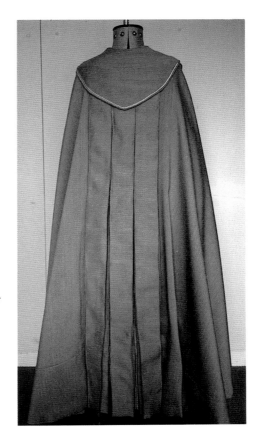

'The Peace Cope', designed and made by Anna Crossley for the Rt. Revd Kilmer Meyers, Bishop of California, Grace Cathedral, San Francisco.

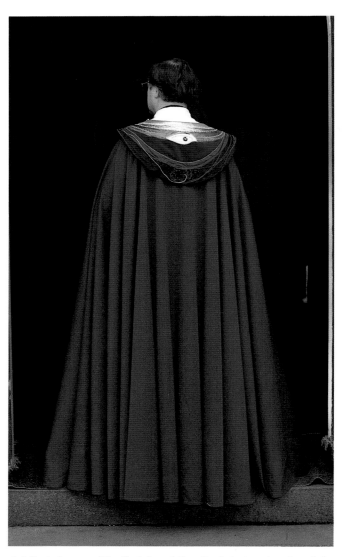

A full-circle cope, 'The first day of Creation', designed and made by Nigel Wright, Melbourne, Australia. Symbolizes the Spirit of God brooding over the waters of chaos. In the centre is an eye, an ancient symbol of God. Woollen and synthetic fabrics embroidered by hand and machine.

The Easter Cope, designed by Polly Hope and embroidered by Leonard Childs and members of the Cathedral Workshop, Derby. The silver clasp was carried out by Michael Hall, of Derby, to Polly Hope's design.

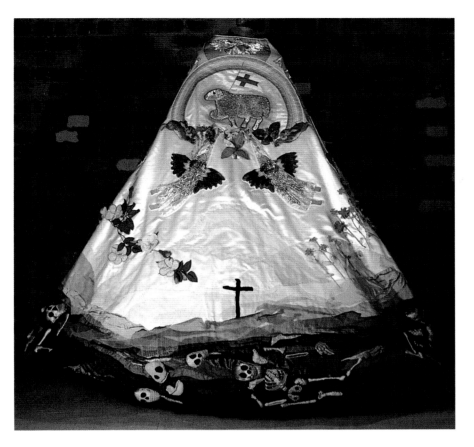

Mitre

The episcopal headdress, ensign of the bishop, is the mitre, but it did not assume the form with which we are now familiar until after the eleventh century in this country. It increased in height until reaching the towering form of the baroque era, now considered decadent. There has been a return to the low mitre where the points may be reduced to right angles (Fig. 13a). The infulae, or lappets, have been retained but are narrower (right), and the cope and mitre are generally alike, but need not conform to the liturgical colours.

Predictable and uninteresting is the traditional decoration of the mitre, consisting of the central orphrey with a band of ornamentation around the head, whereas there can be great scope for originality (Figs. 13b and 13c).

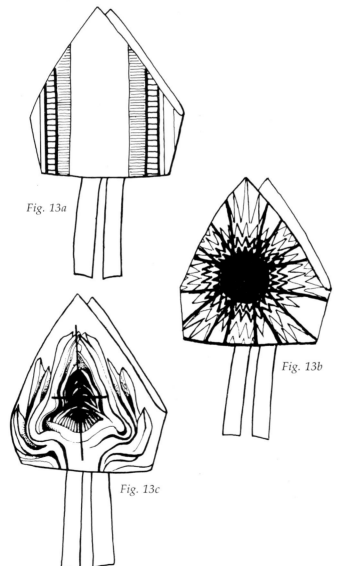

Fig. 13a

Fig. 13b

Fig. 13c

'The Annunciation'. A cope and mitre for Bishop Penny Jamieson, Diocese of Dunedin, New Zealand; the first woman bishop in the Anglican world in charge of her own diocese. Designed by Elizabeth Auton and made by a group of embroiderers.

Mitre (back view), designed and embroidered by Anna Crossley for the Rt. Revd Kilmer Meyers, Bishop of California.

The Red cope and mitre, designed and embroidered by Judith Peacock for the Bishop of Kingston, was to be suitable for many occasions. It was inspired by the words 'Merciful God, you have prepared for those who love you such good things as pass our understanding . . . .' The cope hangs and moves well. The tonal values were achieved with spray-dyeing, transparent fabrics, machine-embroidery and metal threads.

Throw-over altar cloth designed and executed by Belinda Scarlett for Lambeth Palace Chapel, London. Inspired by 'Light – the visible reminder of invisible light' – T. S. Eliot (The Rock IX).

Designing liturgical furnishings

The church as a place of worship plays an important part in the life of a community. Its furnishings should reflect its beliefs, and contribute visually and spiritually to the background of devotional services.

Altar frontals

Traditionally the high altar was placed at the east end of the cathedral or church, although today a free-standing or nave-altar is more usual. This has resulted from the modern liturgical movement, where the emphasis is on the connection between the liturgy and daily life and, consequently, the free-standing altar is preferred. Because the priest faces the people, it may be slightly lower and shorter than usual. Its size and shape will determine the form of the frontal or altar cloth to be used.

The altar symbolizes the earthly triumph of good over evil, so it occupies the most important position visually; indeed, Sir Ninian Comper said, 'I build from the altar outwards.' In the Roman Catholic church it symbolizes the Body of Christ, the altar of sacrifice and also the table of the Last Supper, therefore the design must emphasize these beliefs. More recently canopies have added to the importance of the altar, but there are other ways of achieving the same purpose, for example with an embroidered dossal, or hanging cloth, provided that it is against a wall and will accord well with the whole ambience (p. 82).

If the nave altar is made of wood or stone, there may be a narrower altar cover, or fall, or alternatively there may be a throw-over altar cloth. Where the high altar at the east has been retained, this frontal is frequently mounted on a stretcher.

Designing an altar frontal or cloth presents the most interesting and exciting challenge, and because it is viewed from a distance an understanding of scale is all-important. An appreciation of architecture is vital and will influence the whole concept including the form, and also the colour. Such an example is the altar cloth (p. 11) by Pat Russell for Norwich Cathedral. It is a bold and creative statement which makes a real impact upon the imagination. The approach to this larger scale is more readily realized with the use of machine embroidery, appliqué (p. 45 (bottom)), and dyes and paints (pp. 42 and 47 (top)).

Although practical considerations do play a part in the planning right from the commencement, it is capturing an inspired idea together with the vision to translate that imagery in terms of fabric and stitchery which lifts some of the outstanding contemporary examples into the realm of twentieth-century art. Typical of such examples are the works of Jane Lemon, carried out under her direction by the Sarum group. The 'Energy' frontal (p. 14), and her design based upon the abstraction of the rose, a symbol of Our Lady (p. 15), also the flowing rhythm expressing water in the frontal (p. 44), are superb.

Many of the points stressed in these pages will be discovered by studying the illustrations. Look at the splendid interpretation of the symbolic phoenix

The 'Revelation' frontal, designed and executed in machine and hand-embroidery by Polly Hope, for All Saints, Whitstable, Kent. It is four-sided, each side depicting positive visions and imagery in a lively and decorative way.

by Joan Freeman for St Albans Abbey, worked by Clarissa Robinson (p. 20 (bottom)), and other examples of her interesting use of decorative symbols (p. 19 (bottom left)). Polly Hope's 'Revelation' frontal is unique in the way in which the spirit of the Book of Revelation has been captured in terms of stitched textiles (p. 43).

Belinda Scarlett's inspiration tends to be intellectual and when designing the altar cloth (p. 42) for Lambeth Palace Chapel she was influenced by T.S. Eliot's *The Rock IX:* 'Light – the visible reminder of invisible light'. She explores light as a spiritual image; cosmic light with its creative power and energy radiates from the still centre, while the dove of the Holy Spirit illuminates each human soul with the fire of love.

Although it is often difficult to recollect afterwards what the source of inspiration has been, Belinda Scarlett has most generously shared with us some of her thoughts during the creation of her altar cloth for Winchester Cathedral (p. 6):

Being beyond all being
Existence uncreate
Framer of the Universe.
From the Private Prayers of Lancelot Andrewes,
Bishop of Winchester, 1619–26.

This work celebrates the alliance between religion and conservation.

All things depend on each other and hands are used here to indicate this interdependence. The hands of the Creator suggest a personal, loving God in the act of giving; the hands of man are open to receive and in turn to reciprocate divine love by caring for the creation. We are partners with God; a stewardship is granted, not a licence to abuse, exploit or destroy.

The sun, the supreme cosmic power, is a symbol of God, the source of spiritual light and love.

The river was chosen because of the ancient connection between Winchester and the River Itchen. The otter – an animal in need of our protection – is here. So, too, are the kingfisher, dragonfly, water-lily, frog and fish. A heron takes flight. Water sustains life. Greenness suggests growth, renewal.

The rainbow is a symbol of reconciliation, the meeting of heaven and earth. After the flood God promised not to destroy the earth again and the rainbow was 'the token of the covenant which I make between me and you and every living creature that is with you' (Genesis 9:12).

Darkness suggests infinity, the beyond. On the far side of the altar cloth night is depicted. Reflections in the river reveal the phases of the moon, stars, Saturn. . .a hint of the vastness of the universe. The design was painted with dyes on to a silk background so that layers of colour were built up. Certain areas were then worked into in various ways. Fabrics such as shot silks and gauzes were appliquéd to enhance the reflection of the sun on the water. To achieve the translucent effect of the rainbow a great arc was painted on to a gauze, then pleated along the curves of the arc and appliquéd. The creatures,

'Festal frontal', designed by Jane Lemon for Salisbury Cathedral, and worked by the late Mollie Collins, Catherine Talbot, Jane Lemon and Ann McIntyre. The piece depicts the element of water, which flows over, through and from the Cross.

'Festal frontal', designed and made by Angela Dewar and Gisela Banbury for Truro Cathedral, Cornwall. The background is spray-dyed and the machine-embroidered fronts were made up separately and then mounted on to the main frame.

Laudian frontal for St Faith's Church, North Dulwich, London. Designed and embroidered by hand and machine by Glenys M. Grimwood. The architectural features in the church were used to create a simple design for the High Altar. Welsh flannel and silk appliqué.

for example, the otter, kingfisher and dragonfly, were embroidered by hand. The hands were quilted and appliquéd. Various threads and wools were stitched to suggest the river weed.

Judy Barry and Beryl Patten have carried out a great many excellently designed commissions over the years, for example the frontal for All Saints' Parish Church, Bury (p. 46). Back in 1976 they worked out an interesting set of vestments and a permanent throw-over for Manchester Cathedral. Because of a lack of storage space, they planned an ingenious scheme whereby three panels were created in each of the liturgical colours. These were attached with Velcro, a touch-and-hold fabric fastener, to the frontal and changed according to the season.

To mention just one other example, Leonard Childs thought up an original idea for Southwell Minster; over a basic Laudian frontal an embroidered circle of fabric could be spread, and according to the requirements of the season, it could be replaced by an addition of garlands constructed of flowers and fruit made in a three-dimensional method, which are very attractive.

It is invidious, but unavoidable, that so few works can be mentioned individually and, ideally, every example should be seen in the setting for which it was designed. The frontals shown are typical of many good modern textiles which can be discovered in cathedrals and churches, where the choice has been for an up-to-date creation. There are still instances, of course, where it is fitting that damasks and brocades should be used and when a traditional approach is right. Also, to retain the superfrontal may improve the proportion of some altars, but we now generally prefer the shape of the rectangle, resulting from abandoning the superfrontal.

When contemplating the creation of a design for an altar frontal, there are several points which must be considered. At what stage the 'idea' or inspiration is conceived varies, but the factors listed in Fig. 14, on page 48 all help in adding to the final result.

These are conscious considerations and at some stage the inspiration for the idea will motivate the design. During the briefing, preferences may be suggested, perhaps the inclusion of a special symbol, but if this is not welcome and will not fit into your design, persuasion may be tried! Think about these points in relation to the coloured illustrations shown in this chapter, as they will be of considerable help to you.

As a general guide, the designer should prepare three or four designs, sketched out and presented attractively, together with an estimate and samples of the textiles suggested.

Altar frontal by Judy Barry and Beryl Patten for All Saints' Church, Bury, Lancs.

Altar cloth, designed by Belinda Scarlett for St John the Baptist, Snape, Suffolk. 'God is the still point at the centre' – Julian of Norwich.

Altar frontal developed, from the design of architect Ronald G. Sims, by Rose Walker for the Church of the Holy Redeemer, Acomb, York. When doing her own creative designs she interprets them freely using various techniques.

Design concepts

1. Think about the character of the architecture and this will contribute to determining the type of design which would be most applicable. For example, something along the lines of the altar-cloth design (Fig. 14a) could take its place in a traditional setting. For a modern interior, something abstract could be used (Figs. 14b, 14c, 14g, and 14h). Perhaps the designs shown in Figs. 14d and 14e would be acceptable in an unsophisticated country church.

2. It is important that designs accord with the season, or feast day, and Fig. 14i obviously has a restricted use.

3. Determine the scale: if it is for a cathedral or larger church, the frontal will be viewed from a distance. Larger shapes will make an impact, whereas detail will be lost (Figs. 14a, 14b, 14f, 14g and 14h).

4. Symmetry can be boring, so enliven it by introducing contrasting shapes (Figs. 14d, 14h and 14i). A central motif is dull.

5. A balanced design (Figs. 14b, 14c and 14g), is frequently more interesting and is fun to carry out. Build up to the centre of interest, wherever it is placed. It might be in the form of a vignette.

6. First, plan the basic lines and large shapes (Figs. 14f, 14g and 14h), and detail can be added later.

7. Rhythm and movement should be considered. Sometimes a linear rhythm is needed (Figs. 14a, 14c, 14f and 14g).

8. The choice of colour will generally be spontaneous and related to the ambient. The colours will react to the light and it is essential to try them out in situ; this also applies especially to the fabrics.

9. When it is important that the design shall make an impact, including areas of contrasting tones will help (Figs. 14c, 14g and 14h).

10. In a church planned for corporate worship, with a free-standing or nave altar, a Laudian altar cloth (Fig. 14a) is usually preferred. The corners can be shaped and there are many other examples given. For practical reasons it may be preferable to confine the area of the decoration to the central width of the fabric and the form of the design will determine the positioning of the seams (Figs. 14a and 14i). Should it be mounted on a stretcher, it can be treated as a panel (Figs. 14b, 14c, 14e, 14f, 14g and 14h).

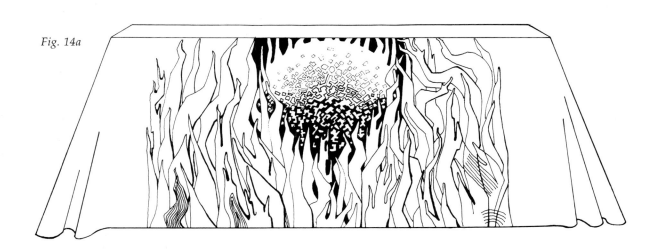

Fig. 14a

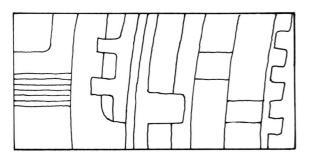

Fig. 14b

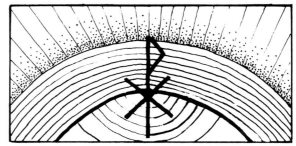

Fig. 14f

Fig. 14c

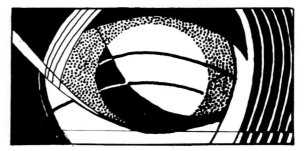

Fig. 14g

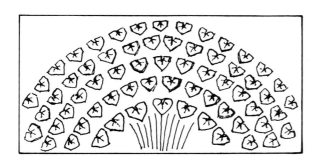

Fig. 14d

Fig. 14h

Fig. 14e

Fig. 14i

Altar linen

Design for altar linen has been somewhat neglected but it could easily be considered on a larger scale and as an abstract format. Shapes filled with drawn-thread and pulled-work textures will contrast with linear stitches, but these techniques require a coarser, or hand-woven linen. The continental custom of working with coloured or neutral threads is interesting, but laundering must remain an important consideration.

Some traditions must be observed, for instance, the fair-linen, which goes over the altar, is usually enriched with wide borders (Fig. 15b) at the ends, which should reach almost to the floor. It should have four small crosses at the corners and one in the centre of the mensa (Fig. 15a), and the credence cloth should match. The corporal, which is square (Fig. 15c), is considered to be very sacred and is kept in the burse. The embroidery is usually worked in the centre of the front and it is folded in three each way. Openwork is unsuitable as particles of the Host might adhere to the cloth.

The pall (Fig. 15d), is made in the form of an envelope, with embroidery in the centre: it is stiffened with a plastic square. The edges can be more interesting if an alternative to hemstitching is used. Interesting drawn-thread borders frequently decorate the surplice and cotta.

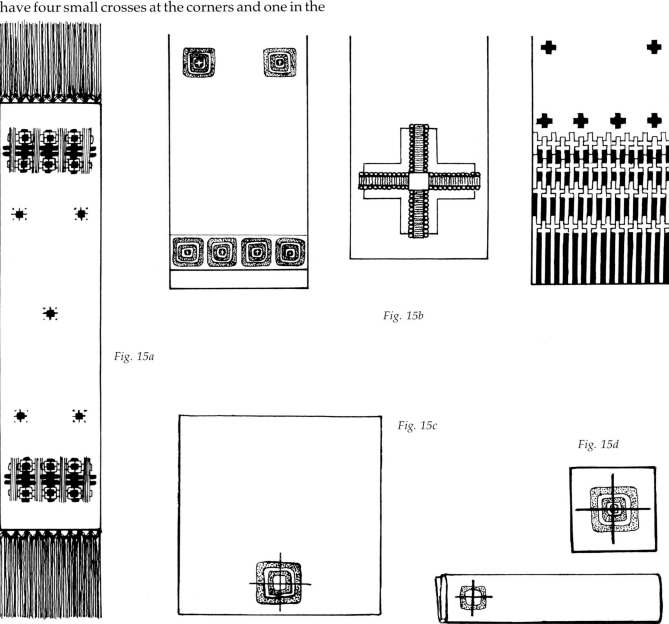

Fig. 15a

Fig. 15b

Fig. 15c

Fig. 15d

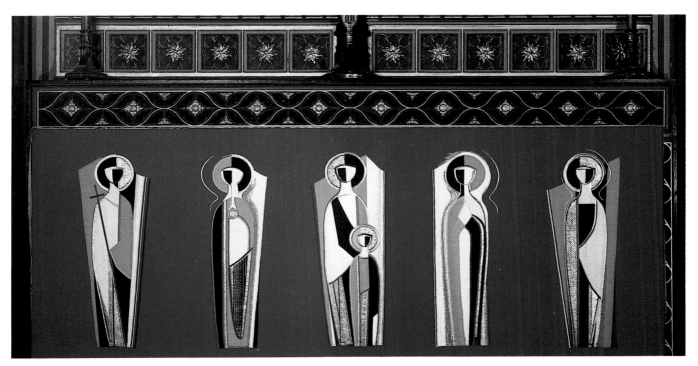

Frontal from St Michael's, Highgate, London. Designed and worked by Sylvia Green, with assistance from members of St Michael's Embroidery Group. The work of the Holy Spirit over human nature is represented by gold, white and purple. The figures suggest the attributes — power to fight evil, prayerfulness, sacrificial love, praise and suffering.

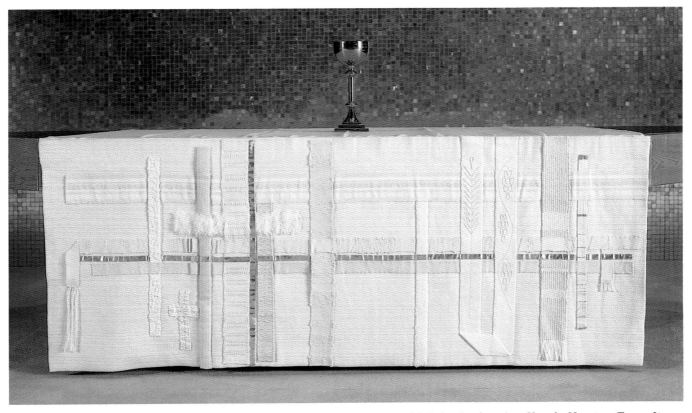

Communion table cloth, for the Memorial Drive Presbyterian Church, Houston, Texas. It was woven by Judy McCalla, Leslie Pretorius and Dottie Williams, who directed the work. The frontal, which is separate and attached with Velcro, is woven in white and off-white pearl cotton random stripes and treadled twill, to which were applied stripes of varied weaves, yarns and materials.

Burse and veil

The burse contains the corporal and the veil covers the chalice (Fig. 16a). The burse generally measures about 23cm (9in) square (Figs. 16b and 16c), and the veil 50 to 60cm (20 to 24in) square (Figs. 16f and 16g), although this can vary according to the height of the chalice (p. 53 (centre right) and Fig. 16a).

The fabric usually matches that of the vestments and conforms to the liturgical colour of the season, but if it is too thick or stiff to drape well, it is unsuitable. A thin, light lining material is used for the veil. To cover the inside of each of the two stiff squares which form the burse plus hinge, white linen should be used.

Whether embroidered by hand or machine, the burse is very interesting to design because there is allowance for a great deal of freedom for technical experimentation (p. 53 (top left and bottom)). Exciting threads, beads, cords, jewels and studs can be employed, even if the result is a bumpy surface. There is really only one limitation to observe and that is to ascertain the practice of the church concerned as to whether, when the burse is standing on the altar, the hinge is on the top or at the side, as this will influence the design (Figs. 16d and 16e).

Traditionally, the veil was usually decorated with a cross in the centre of the front edge; now great latitude is possible, provided that the design relates to the arrangement of the veil when placed over the chalice. The centre can be plain as it is not seen.

Although the burse and veil are not now required, they are still used in some churches.

Fig. 16a

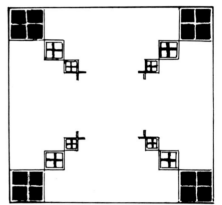

Fig. 16f

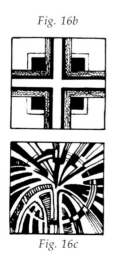

Fig. 16b

Fig. 16c

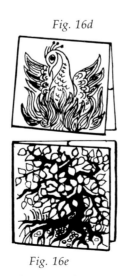

Fig. 16d

Fig. 16e

Fig. 16g

Burse, designed and embroidered by Yvonne Morton. The Chi-Rho evolved from the spokes of a wheel interlaced in cross form; the tooth sprockets became thorns.

Burse, designed and embroidered by Chris Baker, for the small Norman-style village church of All Hallows, East Huntspill, Somerset.

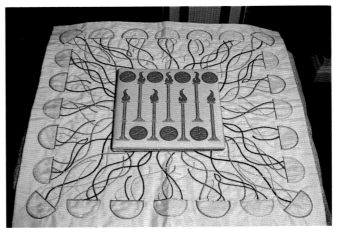

Burse and veil, part of the Red set, designed and embroidered by Leonard Childs and Simon Nelson for the Bishop of Chester.

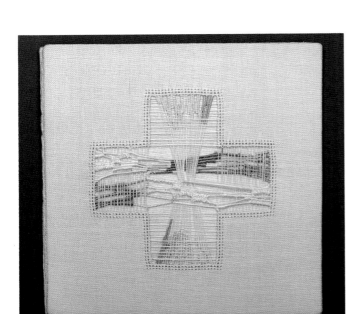

Above and left: *Burse and veil, designed and worked by Elise M. Uttley for All Saints' Church, Sinan, St Asaph, Clwyd. An experiment with drawn threads and needle weaving, resulting in a cross form.*

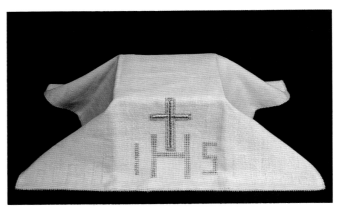

Pulpit falls and casket palls

As a result of the Vatican Council steering guide and the recommendations of the Liturgical Reform Commission, it was decided that the ministry of the words should take place as near to the people as possible: from a lectern or ambo, which is a standing desk for reading and preaching. The ambo represents the dignity and uniqueness of the 'Word of God' and of reflection upon that word. As the liturgical centre for action, well-designed decoration embroidered on a fall should reflect, and relate to, the message.

The pulpit and secondary lectern, should there be one, may have falls which, because of their importance, are generally made considerably longer and possibly wider than usual (Fig. 17a). The introduction of this additional colour, which generally conforms to that of the season, together

The Pillar pulpit fall, designed and executed by Hannah Frew Paterson, for Kilarrow Parish Church, Bowmore, Isle of Islay. The colours of the land beyond and the sky above form the background stripes, on which is placed a gold cross together with a replica of the central supporting pillar of the Round Church.

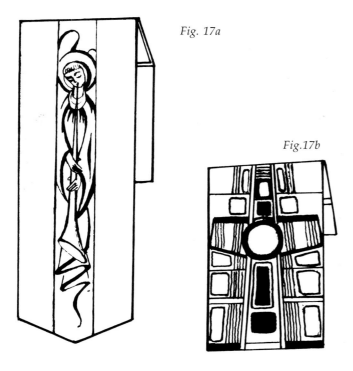

Fig. 17a

Fig.17b

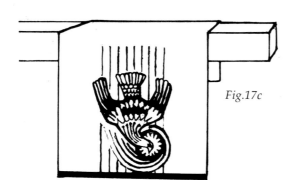

Fig.17c

with a striking design should contribute to the interior decoration, so that these falls become an interesting and important feature in the whole scheme.

Because few technical limitations apply, there is scope for something really exciting. The embroidery can be experimental, even three-dimensional, and the choice of subject for the design is wide. The fall itself hangs from a covered board which is constructed to fit the shape of the desk-top of the pulpit, although the light fittings may present a problem. The fall is attached to the front edge of the board, either by stitching or with strips of velcro fabric fastener (opposite, right and below right, and Fig. 17b). The overall shape of the fall need not be restricted to a rectangle, provided that the proportions are satisfactory. In fact, many falls are now made from quite large horizontal rectangles.

A funeral pall (known in America as a casket pall) is often official, so the design may be heraldic, and it is made up in the same way as a Laudian, or throw-over frontal. The measurements have to be ascertained, as this affects the design. Some priests request a design for the pall which is also suitable for use as a hanging at Easter. This may make the choice of symbolic meaning difficult to reflect in the design (p. 54 (bottom).

Altar covers hang almost to the ground, or are slightly shorter. They are similar to the lectern cover and are made in the same way (Fig. 17c), and measure about 90 x 190cm (36 x 76in).

Above right: *Pulpit fall, designed and machine-embroidered by Hannah Frew Paterson. The triangular repeating units are based upon the roof support beams of St Mary's Church, Motherwell, Lanarkshire, which is associated with the steel industry. From the square which represents the dying furnace, the eye is led upwards to the Dove of Hope.*

Right: *Pulpit fall, designed and worked by Cheryl Sly, Department of Textiles, Glasgow School of Art. The shipbuilding of Greenock provided the inspiration whilst the colour tones echo the arrangement of organ pipes in the Mid Kirk of Greenock.*

Opposite: *Funeral pall (a casket pall in the USA). Sometimes these palls are used as Easter hangings. Designed and made by Beryl Dean for St Mark's Church, Philadelphia. Produced in patchwork and appliqué.*

DESIGNING BANNERS AND PENNANTS

With the relocation of liturgical space, banners and hangings have become increasingly important as a means of introducing colour and interest to those areas no longer in use. This is a return to the medieval practice of bringing out the long banners and pennants at festival times. To quote from the committee of bishops on the liturgy (1978) 'they invite . . . temporary decoration for particular celebrations, feasts and seasons. Banners and hangings of various sorts are both popular and appropriate, as long as the nature of these forms is respected. They are creations composed of forms, colours and textures, rather than signboards to which words must be attached. Their purpose is to appeal to the senses and thereby create an atmosphere and a mood, rather than to impress a slogan upon the mind of the observer, or deliver a verbal message.' The series of banners carried out in dyed painting by Thetis Blacker for Winchester Cathedral are a notable example.

Interest is now growing in the use of hangings and a realization of their value in a decorative scheme. Designing a banner is a challenge, because the attention of the viewer must be attracted and the impact quickly established, so that the message is conveyed in an impression gained however fleetingly, perhaps as a procession moves away. To have the lettering on the reverse side draws attention to the back of the banner, as it may be seen for longer than the front. When designing the banner (p. 57), Ruth Tudor felt strongly that a banner should be two-sided. Her brief included 'A Mother and Child', the Mothers' Union Logo and the Tavistock Coat of Arms, together with the arms of the See. Mainly machine embroidery on Indian dupion silks was used in the construction.

A design for a banner needs to be straightforward, and is generally based upon a figurative subject, interpreted creatively, strongly, and in an interesting way. Secondary subjects, and too much detail, detract from the main impact and the scale should be fairly large. Meaningless orphreys, ornament-ation, machine-made fringes and other elaborations only take away from the main impression. Good, legible lettering is essential (pp. 86 and 87).

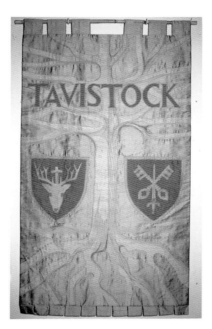

A double-sided banner, designed and executed, mainly in machine-embroidery, by Ruth Tudor for Tavistock church.

Opposite: *One of four pennants, part of a project for All Saints', Newland, Gloucestershire, designed by Sylvia Green and carried out by Mary Brooks*

The Golden Section is a guide to the proportion of the rectangle, although the width may be determined by an existing banner pole, which should not be too heavy. If possible, a pole especially designed for the banner is an advantage. The loops from which it is suspended are spaced with a gap in the centre for the fitment.

It is important to consider carefully the surroundings against which the banner will be seen when it is not in use. Judy Barry and Beryl Patten tried out various fabrics and several sizes of lettering before making the final decision (p. 58 (top right)). The background against which a choir banner is permanently viewed should influence its design and colour.

As the subject for banners, hangings, panels and falls the human form is the basis for much design which depends upon a formalized and decorative interpretation (above, pp. 7, 58 (bottom), and 87 (bottom)). So many Mothers' Union banners are sentimental and too realistic to be treated in a really exciting and experimental way, but Margaret Nicholson has opened up some new approaches, as did Beryl Dean's book in 1952 with the Golden Banner for Chelmsford Cathedral. The whole field is much broader than it was, and now includes all kinds of fabric, hand- and machine-stitched effects, metal threads, dyes and paints, and today these methods are all acceptable (p. 58 (left)).

The many variations upon traditional techniques can add interest by introducing a fresh approach to the treatment of figure subjects in ecclesiastical embroidery. By constantly observing interesting ways of treating the human form decoratively, it is possible to discover new interpretations (p. 72), and these can be applied to banners. It requires a great deal of thought to incorporate a really typically modern work into a very dated interior, but the experienced designer will persevere until it is made to harmonize. It is important that no discordant embroidery should be introduced.

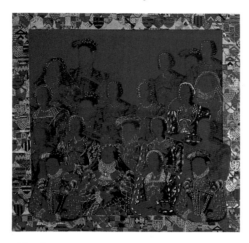

'The Congregation', designed and executed by Val Porter. Screen printed figures on a red ground with hand- and machine-embroidery in metallic threads; appliqué and reverse appliqué, the fabric being cut back to several metallic nets; laces; beads; and panels for the areas of adornment. The frame is of bleached, varnished and screen-printed tissue, mixed wool and cotton fabrics and interfaces, padded and machined with metal threads.

The inspiration for the panel above came while Val Porter was studying slashing on garments, during her wide research for the ecclesiastical and heraldic sections of City and Guilds which she took at the London College of Fashion. She says she has 'become passionately interested in the subject and in the relationship of a range of materials for expressing an idea, and the possibilities of combining traditional techniques in an unexpected way with transfer dyes, screen printing and bleach on tissues or fabric to give a variety of surface qualities.' This approach makes her work applicable to the creation of banners, hangings or frontals. She likes 'to extend the embroidery on to the frame, mount or border', and she also 'considers the idea of the juxtaposing of different materials to create a similar effect.'

The introduction of pennants would bring colour into many a dark church, and it is so regrettable that this form of decoration is rather neglected. But at the

Mothers' Union banner, shown in situ, designed and carried out by Judy Barry and Beryl Patten in 1983 for the Radcliffe and Prestwich Deanery Mothers' Union. During the interpretation of the design into fabric, the surroundings were considered and alterations were made to the size of the lettering.

Banner, designed by Peter Hinchcliffe, machine-embroidered, and spray-dyed by Gillian Alexandra Smith for the Mothers' Union, Chelmsford Cathedral, Essex.

Banner for St Barnabas-on-the-desert, Paradise Valley, Arizona, designed and worked by Lee Porzio in dupion and similar-weight silks in desert colours. The prevailing sun, also a symbol for Christ, the arid earth covered with a large isolated bloom, and the bold arch based on the arched walkway of the church – all reflect the work of the disciple who is called the bridge between the Old and New Testament.

Hanging, 'Our Lord the Healer', designed and executed by Pat Iles, for the Chapel of Healing at Whitehill Close, Borden, Hampshire.

lovely old church known locally as 'The Cathedral of the Forest', at Newland in Gloucestershire, they had the imagination to commission a most exciting project which included a set of pennants, one of which is shown at page 56.

Hangings and panels

Hangings can play a very important part in enhancing the interior of a place of worship, by making it more interesting through the introduction of colour; this may be in the form of a dossal, linking it with the frontal. A commission to undertake a hanging or panel is really exciting because there is usually latitude in the design and great scope for originality in the approach to creating a striking composition. This can be carried out with the ingenious exploration of hand and machine stitchery and the discovery of unusual textiles. A strong design is essential, as it will probably become a focal point.

Many interesting hangings and panels have been created in terms of textile and stitch, but it is only possible to include a few examples here. On a really huge scale is Hannah Frew Patterson's panel for the church at Cardross. Two smaller pieces of her work are the pulpit falls (pp. 54 (top), 55 (top)). Kath Whyte will also be remembered for her large examples of ecclesiastical embroidery. Pamela Pavitt has expressed meaningful ideas through her panels; page 62 (top) is one example. Judy Barry and Beryl Patten have produced many striking wall hangings (p. 61). These show their approach to building up and developing the design to be carried out in appliqué on a large scale. The scope and versatility shown in the embroideries created by Polly Hope may be judged from the few examples included (pp. 12, 43, 90, 91). The outstanding panel commissioned for a crematorium designed and carried out by Eleri Mills (p. 60) exemplifies the very special and unique characteristics which can be achieved with stitched textiles.

The experienced designer exercises discrimination when planning a panel which is to be introduced into an existing scheme, as it is essential that it should harmonize. Through her imaginative use of textiles, Rozanne Hawksley expresses something beyond that which is usually achievable. She may create a haunting quality or an ironic theme, seldom associated with needle arts (p. 62 (bottom)).

This striking panel, designed and worked by Eleri Mills, was commissioned by Poole Borough Council for the crematorium. It was inspired by the dramatic setting, with walls which sweep upwards to form a lofty triangular point. It was hoped that each visitor, as the eye travelled upwards, would find expression for their own thoughts. The architect concerned did involve Eleri in the scheme and the spirit of the design was evoked by the architecture. The work was carried out in paint, hand-stitching and appliqué.

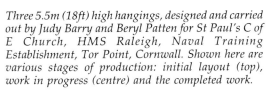

Three 5.5m (18ft) high hangings, designed and carried out by Judy Barry and Beryl Patten for St Paul's C of E Church, HMS Raleigh, Naval Training Establishment, Tor Point, Cornwall. Shown here are various stages of production: initial layout (top), work in progress (centre) and the completed work.

61

Bicentenary panels for Hinde Street Church and West London Mission, whose symbol is the Cross and Dove in Hand. Designed and carried out by Pamela Pavitt and Pat Cove, with assistance from Croydon Embroiderers' Guild. The rainbow colours represent hope and the hands and people suggest mission.

A panel, '. . . casualties were surprisingly light. . .', created by Rozanne Hawksley in 1991. An installation/memorial to the first seventeen dead brought home to the UK, via RAF Brize Norton, from the Gulf War. Seventeen rough wooden crosses 2m (7ft) high are bolted on to a grid of similar wood; each cross is bagged in cotton canvas, roped and labelled. Three bare crosses, the central one having a crown of thorns, are at the back of the piece, separate from the grid. The work is now permanently in the Museum of Textiles, Poland.

Set of four hangings, designed and carried out by Judy Barry and Beryl Patten for the Fire Service College Commemorative Chapel, in the Officers' Training Establishment, Moreton-in-Marsh, Gloucestershire.

DESIGNING KNEELERS AND ALMS-BAGS

When contemplating the creation of designs for a set of kneelers, it is the mental concept of the total effect produced by repetition which is important, while remembering that each individual design unit must be interesting in itself. This is such a wonderful opportunity to plan a blaze of colour which is to be viewed at floor level, where this is appropriate, or, alternatively, something subtle when this is applicable. A striking effect is so often missed because the importance of the scheme as a visual whole has been overlooked, and the result is dull and undistinguished. Even the individual kneelers may be trivial in concept. It is regrettable that so often much precious time, skill and money may have been wasted because of a lack of judgement in regard to the choice of design.

For kneelers, hassocks and cushions, canvas and wools are used because of their strength and inherent durability, also the ability to withstand dirt, which is essential. The embroidery technique thus imposes its own limitations upon the design; long flowing lines are unsatisfactory, and the shapes tend to become geometrical and angular. The size of the canvas selected should relate to the scale of the design. However, there is a vast variety of decorative stitches, endlessly fascinating to work, and delightful as patterning and texture. Areas of contrasting textures create interest in themselves.

The communicants' rail kneeler presents practical problems which affect the planning of the design, as it is almost impossible to work it in one length. If divided into two sections, the centre may be spoilt by the join, so to have it divided up as three cushions may be more satisfactory. It is possible to join canvas, but not advisable. The communicants' rail kneeler (below), was designed by Frank Stanton for the village church at Kenton. It illustrates the use of symbolism and the effect of brilliant colour.

It is unsuitable to base the decoration for hassocks or kneelers upon the cross or a symbol of God, as it seems wrong to stand or kneel on these symbols, even in prayer. Kneelers, cushions, and other objects require designs related to their shape and purpose. Canvas-work (tapestry is a misnomer, as it is woven

Right: Kneeler, designed by Norma Tallin and worked by Vera Knights and Emma Peck, for All Saints' Church, Kenton, Suffolk.

Below: The Kenton communion kneeler, from All Saints' Church, Kenton, Suffolk. It was designed by Frank Stanton in 1984, and executed by Vera Knights, in the theme of 'The Creation of the World' – Genesis 1. The piece, in two sections, shows the days of creation: dividing light from darkness; dividing the firmaments; separation of earth and water, sowing of seed, yielding of fruits; creation of sun, moon, stars and seasons; creation of creatures in the sea and air; creation of cattle and animals; and finally 'Male and female created He them'.

on a loom) is a suitable technique to use, but it is the effect of repetition which must be considered.

An outstanding example of the variety, interest and standard of technique displayed in canvas-work and stitched textiles is the schemes designed and directed by Sylvia Green for St Michael's Church, Highgate, and worked by a group of people taught by her; two examples are shown below and right. Quite different and equally interesting are the hassocks (and much else) designed and directed by Reverend Leonard Childs and carried out by the Derby Cathedral Workshop and Durham Cathedral Broderers' Guild (above right).

Above: Kneeler, designed by Leonard Childs and worked by The Durham Cathedral Broderers' Guild. The designed lettering commemorates the Saints to whom the Nine Altars Chapel in Durham Cathedral was dedicated in pre-Reformation times.

Below: Cushion, 'The Nativity'. Another example designed by Sylvia Green for St Michael's Church, Highgate, London. This one was stitched by Eleanor Close.

Below right: Phoenix kneeler, designed by Margaret K. Wright for St Edmund's Church, Hardingstone, Northamptonshire.

Below: A cushion, entitled 'The City', is one of many examples designed by Sylvia Green and stitched by Mary Hall. It was made for St Michael's Church, Highgate, London.

Alms-bags

There is scope for much variation in designing alms-bags and considerable latitude when choosing the type of decoration, colour and technique. The shape must obviously depend upon its fitness for the purpose. Of basic importance is its strength, as the bags have to withstand hard wear, and they do get grubby, consequently the choice of fabric and type of embroidery is important.

When planning the shape of a flat bag (see examples opposite), it is necessary to ascertain the capacity required as this will depend upon the number of envelopes and coins estimated for each. This also applies to the size of collecting bags attached to a mount. Having made a pattern, it is advisable to construct a mock-up to try out the capacity and position for the decoration. Existing mounts are generally very old-fashioned, but it is possible to devise an interesting alternative and to get a set made (see example below).

For stitched decoration, canvas-work is practical if worked upon very fine canvas. The result will be clumsy, however, if the stitching extends into the turnings. Fine wool, silk or stranded cotton can be used. Many hand- and machine-embroidery methods are suitable if they will withstand hard wear. A commission (p. 67 (bottom right)), carried out by Louise MacMillan in machine embroidery on soft leather is a perfect example of durability. Thin leather should also be used for lining alms-bags.

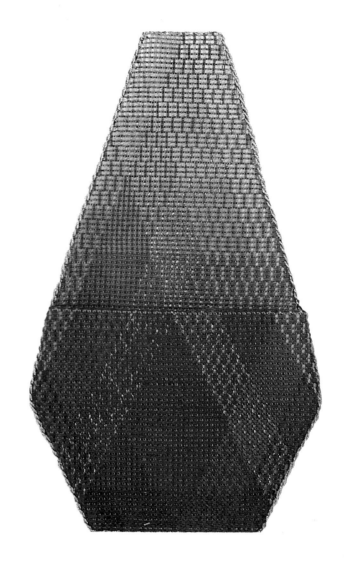

Alms-bag in patchwork with mount, designed by Beryl Dean.

Left and right: A pair of decorative alms-bags, designed and hand-embroidered by Ann Rutherford.

Below left: Alms-bag, designed and machine-embroidered by Pamela Pavitt. Creation based upon the shape of an egg.

Below right: Alms-bag, machine-embroidered on soft leather. This is a very practical idea by Louise MacMillan.

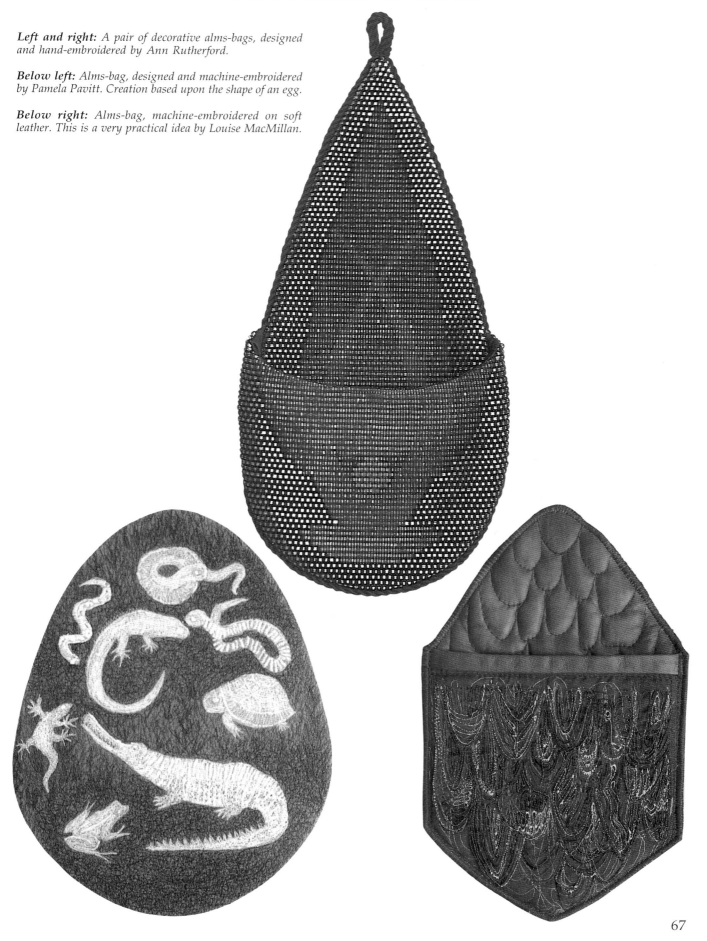

DESIGNING WITH TECHNIQUES

The symbolism attached to gold and other precious metals associated with ecclesiastical embroidery ensures the continuation of this characteristic which is so typical of, but not exclusive to, stitchery for religious purposes (p. 70). As a result of the increased range of synthetic metallic textiles and threads, combined with the experimental derivations from traditional techniques, there is a widening in the interchange of ideas between church and secular embroidery. Also, the scope and inventiveness of machine embroidery is developing all the time. This inevitably influences the way in which a concept is expressed, and fashion, too, will have a bearing upon the outcome, although the creative process is unique to each individual.

The introduction of spraying with dyes and paints, also other experiments, have widened the field of possible effects. But it is a matter of speculation, however, whether the result of painting and spraying on fabrics may ultimately be detrimental to their longevity, although when thinking in secular terms, we are used to accepting expendability. The use of dyes and paints is certainly quicker than, say, applying layers of transparent organzas, but it cannot replace the subtle effect which is thus produced.

When considering the medium to be employed if a flat surface is required, appliqué is almost synonymous with hangings, frontals, altar cloths and copes, because of its suitability for dealing with the large scale needed. Additional interest can be introduced by using metallic fabrics (p. 75 (below left)), and working surface patternings in a variety of ways, mainly by machine.

There are endless possibilities to be explored when hand-loom weaving is used not only as a background but for braids and trimmings. Patchwork may also be developed in many interesting ways (p. 17), so that the beauty of the fabrics is exploited.

In hand embroidery, the skill required to manipulate metal threads is specialized and has developed from experimenting with traditional techniques which depend upon the nature of particular threads. For example, underside couching, so typical of Opus Anglicanum, could only have been executed with the particular thread available at that time, composed of a metal-covered silken core, similar to passing thread, producing the pliancy which has given the work its longevity. The linen sewing thread was taken over the metal thread and through the two layers of handwoven linen and, possibly, an outer layer of silk to continue for the next stitch. Surface couching eventually replaced this method and was used exclusively when Japanese gold was introduced. Many variations of patterning were created by allowing the metal thread to remain on the surface, and it was taken over rows of string or felt that had been sewn down using a strong thread to stitch the metal between the string. Two alternative ways of working basket-stitch filling are shown below (Fig. 18a). One example of a traditional technique which has been adapted to modern requirements is seen at Fig 18b, enlarging the scale of the effect by using a combination of gold plate, narrow velvet ribbon, silk and metal cords, threads and leather thongs.

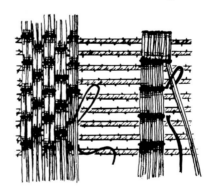

Fig. 18a

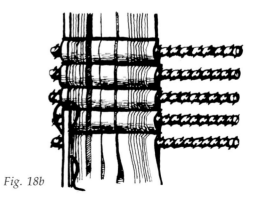

Fig. 18b

Burden stitch can be adapted to present-day needs by laying the long foundation stitches in a thicker metal thread, which are then worked over with silk, metal thread or short lengths of purl (Fig. 19).

Fig.19

There are many variations, and by using padding, the metal threads are highlighted, and a basic traditional method is shown (Fig. 20a). There are many possibilities of changing the effects by experimenting with different ways of making raised shapes. In Fig. 20b, the padding is stuck down and the gold plate, or an alternative strip, is sewn with a coloured thread which enhances the effect.

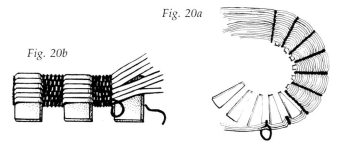

Fig. 20a

Fig. 20b

It is possible to stitch many surface patterns by hand or machine, and Fig. 21 is an example.

Fig. 21

Cords sewn to make all-over textures will also break up the flatness of appliqué, if this is required. Gold, silver or coloured purls and bullion form exciting textures and these techniques are being introduced into present-day embroideries (Fig. 22).

Fig. 22

Tubular braids, cords and rat-tails, when sewn down, produce characteristically flowing lines (Fig. 23)

Fig. 23

Couching down threads and cords of varying thicknesses can also be interesting (Fig. 24). By machine stitching with contrasting threads, either linear patterns can be produced or, with repetition, areas of surface textures can be invented. The various knotted stitches, or applied beads and studs, all add to the interest of the surface, as do pure wool, silk yarns and an unexpected introduction of coloured lurex (p. 75 (bottom left)).

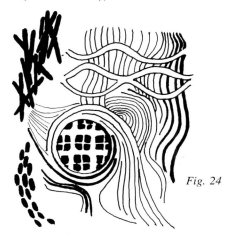

Fig. 24

An appreciation of the subtle differences in gold and coloured metal threads can be developed by juxtaposing them (p. 75 (right)). The effect will be heightened by stitching with coloured threads and introducing padding.

In the hands of artists, embroidery has developed in ways undreamed of some years ago and themes charged with feeling are created, in which the actual textural quality of the stitchery produces the idea being sought in the imagination. The panel by Eleri Mills (p. 73 (bottom)) possesses these qualities. When undertaking work for the church there is scope for this sensitive approach, in fact religion should engender these creative ideas, but it is a pity that so much is nothing but mere decoration. Rozanne Hawksley's works are wonderful examples which evoke emotions through the choice of subject and imaginative treatment. The themes depicted are expressed in terms of fabric and technique to which one responds (p. 62 (bottom)).

Figurative subjects

The human figure frequently features in religious design, and the imagery reflects the ideas which are typical of the time, while the whole concept is communicated visually. It is important, however, to consider the medium in which the subject will be carried out, as this will influence the approach to the design. The figure must be seen in relation to the work as a whole, and thought of primarily as a shape, having rhythm and character. It must also be of a scale which fits happily into the shape it is to fill and have an empathy with the surroundings.

Each embroidered head shown here is but one example illustrating a technique chosen as best

expressing the original concept. For the icon, below, the use of Japanese gold and the skill required were intended to convey the sanctity of the subject. Margaret Nicholson has treated this traditional technique in a new way (p. 71 (bottom left)). Quite different in character is 'The Mother and Child' by Gisela Banbury, top right. It was created in appliqué, hand and machine-embroidery. The 'White Madonna' (p. 71 (bottom right)) is an example of solid hand stitchery worked with a variety of direction and tension to sculpt the surface into low relief, exploiting the play of light on the shiny nylon thread. Barbara Siedlecka has also carried out a head entitled 'Miner'

'Head of Christ', designed and worked by Beryl Dean in the method now known as or nué. *Japanese gold thread and filoselle silks were used. This is a revival of the traditional technique.*

Detail from 'Adoration', the third of five panels, each measuring 2.7 x 1.2m (9 x 4ft). Designed and hand-embroidered by Beryl Dean for St George's Chapel, Windsor Castle in 1972.

Decorative head, designed and executed by Margaret Nicholson. Adaptation of the traditional method or nué.

'Mother and Child', designed and carried out by Gisela Banbury, in appliqué, hand and machine-stitching.

'White Madonna', a portrait in one thread. Created by Barbara Siedlecka.

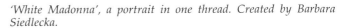

entitled 'Miner' which she quilted with a continuous machined line which shows another interpretation of a head. This is an interesting subject to pursue and when technique is allowed to impose its influence upon the design, it will often add character. For example, the continuous linear quality of tubular braids, cords, gold, and machine stitching can often result in decorative treatments of the human form evolving.

The five large panels commissioned for the Rutland Chantry, St George's Chapel, Windsor Castle, illustrated incidents from the New Testament and were intended to be recognizable, therefore Beryl Dean worked the heads and hands in long and short stitch, following the modelling of the features with the direction of the stitches. Linen and woollen threads were used (p. 71 (top left)).

Sylvia Green's approach to designing the saints on the red frontal for St Michael's, Highgate, is abstract (p. 51 (top)). It is also interesting to note the difference between the interpretation of the figure on the banner by Ruth Tudor (p. 57), and that of Gillian Smith (p. 58 (bottom)).

Figures to be carried out in quilting should be planned with simplicity. Quite different is the conventional formalization imposed by canvas-work (pp. 64 (right) and 65 (centre right)).

'Saintly Knight', designed and machine-embroidered by Penny Butterworth. One of a series of various permutations.

'Piraeus Harbour', created by Barbara Siedlecka. Dried vegetation, fabrics, fibres, lace netting embedded in paper pulp with added pigments.

Panel produced by Eleri Mills in 1985. Cotton, linen and silk appliqué. Hand-stitched in linen, cotton, rayon and metal threads, acrylic paint. An example of stitched textures forming design.

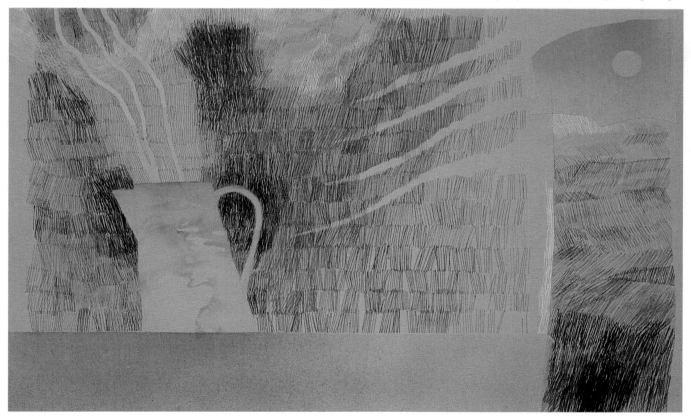

Developments in machine embroidery

Penny Butterworth studied at Windsor and at the London College of Fashion. She specialises in machine embroidery and, being an enthusiast, she follows up the latest developments. She designed and worked 'Saintly Knight' (p. 72), of which she says, 'Interestingly the Medieval/Elizabethan pseudo background of tulips was worked on a swing-needle sewing machine and its accompanying scanner, with memory cards which are fed into it; the pre-set designs are then stitched automatically. The tulips in the background are an example of a motif carried out in this way. The scanner will transfer a design up to 5cm (2in) square on to a card which is then slotted into the machine and stitched.

'At present the only potentially ecclesiastical subject is a bunch of grapes 6cm (2½in) square, but in the hands of able designers these devices can be adapted to produce interesting stitched decoration for the church. There are immense possibilities, but the success depends upon the taste and imagination of the operator. For larger objects mechanical repetition can be used, or several motifs can be linked together. The orientation can be changed and the stitchery stopped during its cycle to change colours. Applied hand stitching then enhances the effect. Four designs at any one time can be put on to the card, so that colour separation takes place and multi-coloured motifs are produced.

Many permutations can be carried out by drawing, then scanning the drawing in outline, making it solid or using the negative image on the scanner for both (Fig. 25) then trying each out in different colour combinations. By using the 20% reduction mode in the scanner all the devices can be made smaller or larger, as required (Fig. 26).

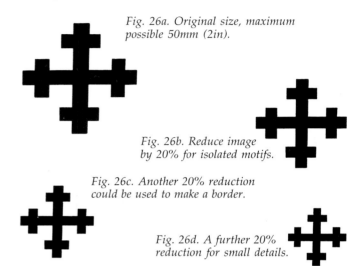

Fig. 26a. Original size, maximum possible 50mm (2in).

Fig. 26b. Reduce image by 20% for isolated motifs.

Fig. 26c. Another 20% reduction could be used to make a border.

Fig. 26d. A further 20% reduction for small details.

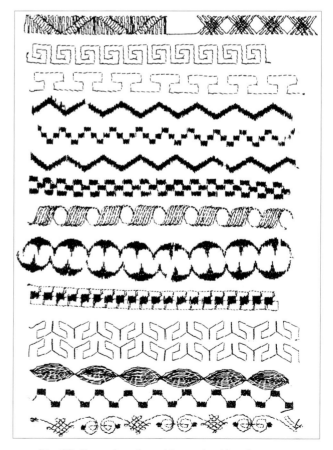

Fig. 27. Examples of machine-embroidered patterns.

Fig. 25. Variations of one design can be used for different purposes.

Any modern swing-needle machine can be used to stitch automatic patterns which are decorative and will withstand laundering in washing machines. The stitch length and width can be altered to change the effect, and several patterns can be used in conjunction, to form composite patterns. These machines with set stitch-patterns are useful for making borders on altar linen (Fig. 27), and if the fabric is of a loose weave, drawn- and pulled-thread work can be simulated.

A combination of exciting textures for large-scale effects, suitable for frontals, banners and hangings, can be produced on these machines by layering the stitch-patterns and using a variety of threads, some to reflect light in different ways.'

Below left: Pulpit fall, designed and carried out by Irene Waller, as part of a set for Cradley Heath Parish Church, West Midlands. Appliqué, using variously textured metallic fabrics and threads.

Bottom left: Detail from Laudian altar. Covering designed, woven and embroidered by Irene Waller for the Blue-coat School, Edgbaston, Birmingham.

Below: Stole, designed by Sylvia Green to develop the juxtaposition of variously coloured gold threads and techniques, and worked by Pamela Waterworth.

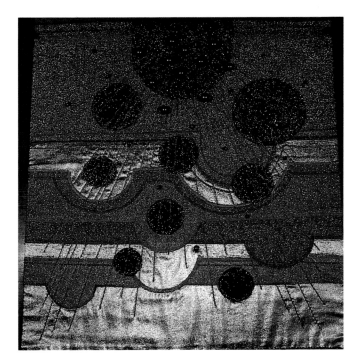

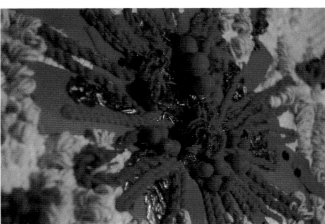

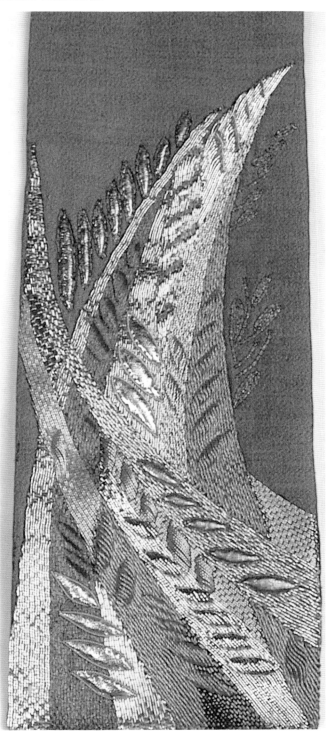

Interpreting design in terms of technique

Many years ago courses for ecclesiastical embroidery were pioneered at the then Hammersmith School of Art, exploring new ways with traditional techniques in the interpretation of good up-to-date designs. The subject is now seriously studied and the whole approach has developed tremendously. The work now done in many colleges and schools has had a widespread and important influence. One such centre is the London College of Fashion, where Anthea Godfrey has initiated a stimulating course

which includes the many elements that combine to create the designs typical of stitched textiles for the church of today. The development of machine embroidery continues to increase, together with the various hand techniques. Anne Raphael has written about some of the exercises from that course and has kindly allowed her work to be reproduced on the following pages, together with some pertinent remarks.

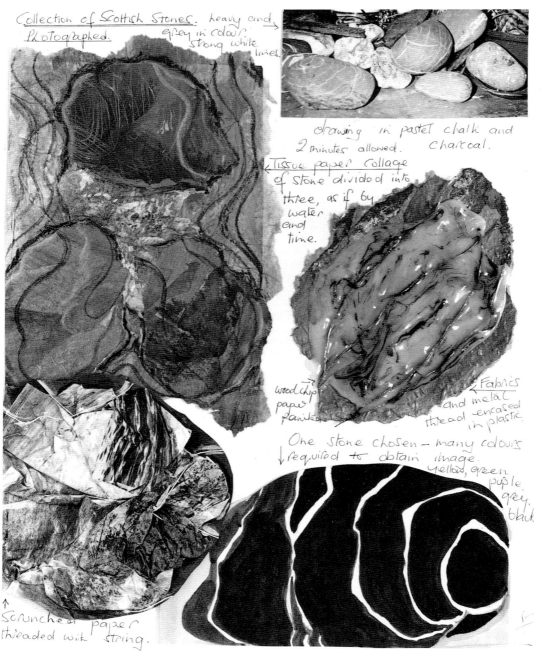

Page from Anne Raphael's sketchbook for 'Scottish Stones'.

Illustrated on these pages is 'Scottish Stones', which depicts time passing and the movement of water.

'Three minutes were allowed to sketch these large heavy grey and white stones. From my drawings and paper experiments, many samples developed.

'I discovered by trial and error that numerous colours were required to create the overall grey tones. Blues, purples, greens, yellow, black, brown and red. This suggested to me the many millions of years that had passed. Also, tidal movements created the shapes.

'As I broke down these colours on paper and fabric, my experiments with stitchery took on a fluid nature.

'Choosing rouleaux made from space-dyed fabric, threads and gold cords gave strength to the movement in a way that single threads did not. Handmade clear plastic, incorporating threads and metal, suggested water.

'Fragmenting the one solid stone into its three main facets, as if by the action of water and time, enabled me to stitch a flat panel.'

'Scottish Stones', by Anne Raphael. Incorporating rouleaux made out of space-dyed fabric, gold cords and thread, hand-made plastic incorporating metal, quilted pieces with cords, and hand-made paper stones with machine-embroidery using Madeira metal threads.

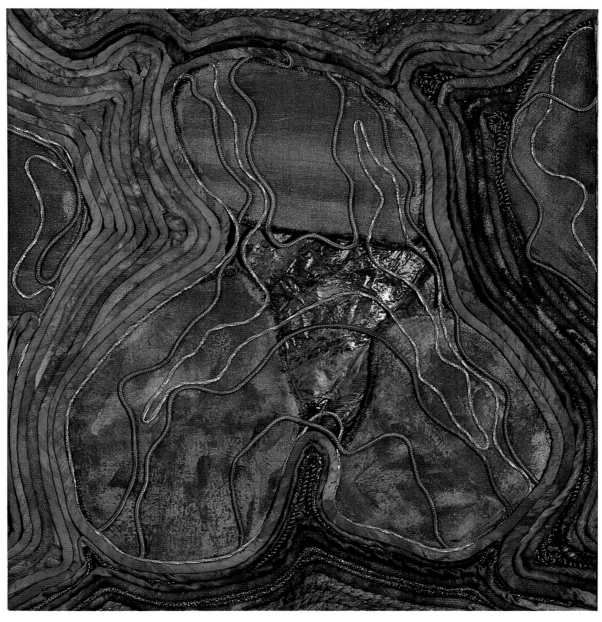

Layered paper and card, torn and painted

Sketch of tree trunk
Black and gold inks, pencil and chalk.

Cords metal threads chain sts. Knots beads.

Photographic Source.

Ink and crayon sketch

Simplified sketch for design
← main → Trunk
Coloured silk
grasses ← water →
← shadows →

Pencil and ink wash on coloured paper.
Bubble print for water surface; ink and pencil.

↑ Tree bark textures ↓

Tree bark
Sketched in Wales.
Water colour and pastel.

Shadow work quilted silk.

Painted silk. or machine lace.

Page from Anne Raphael's sketchbook for 'Pools and Reflections'.

Shown here is 'Pools and Reflections', from studies, drawings and photographs using metal threads.

'Pools, ponds and river banks were studied in detail one spring and summer, and again during winter snow, frosts and moonlight.

'I made the finished piece using the winter studies, feeling the richer threads more suitable for the cold and moonlight. The tiny photograph chosen for the good reflections shown was the final inspiration. A grey-green silk background was washed with fabric paints. Layers of sheer fabrics, chiffon and gauze, were coloured using transfer dyes, creating a variation in colour density. Metallic fabrics and felt were sandwiched in between these layers to create depth and distance. Padded leathers and small beads defined the water line. Grasses and foliage, using pure silk threads in straight stitches, drew the whole together. Free smocking, knotted ribbons, cords, silver threads, chain and knot stitches in perle gave the tree trunks texture.'

'Pools and Reflections', by Anne Raphael. Layers of spray-painted fabrics: felt and metallic fabrics were used, together with ruched silver ribbon, padded leather, metal threads laid traditionally, and metal beads.

Later Anne Raphael was commissioned to create a set of green vestments for the Church of Holy Innocents, Hammersmith, London.

'This large Victorian church was to be gutted and reordered to make a multi-purpose building, providing a large area for worship, great in height and scale. The vicar had two requests in the briefing for the design: (a) it must all be growing, and (b) could the small grape-and-leaf design from the Lady Chapel window be incorporated, as it was a Burne-Jones.

'I spent days in the almost-ruined building sketching, photographing and studying the new plans. The sanctuary was to be the huge stage for the great drama of the Eucharist and my design and work must match this. The old building provided great inspiration

– tiles, carvings, stonework, brick patterns and triangular designs.

'These were the ideas for a free-floating back panel to carry the main designs of grapes, corn and a lily to represent, as a symbol of purity, the first Holy Innocents.

'The component parts of the design were made separately using hand and machine-embroidery on dyed fabrics. For the chasuble, pale gold silk for the free-hanging back triangle was hand-dyed from blue-green at the base to bright gold at shoulder level and down the front, moving over the green linen and suggesting growth. Embroidery at the base of the silk represents the earth, metal threads create highlights and small *or nué* slips add texture and richness.'

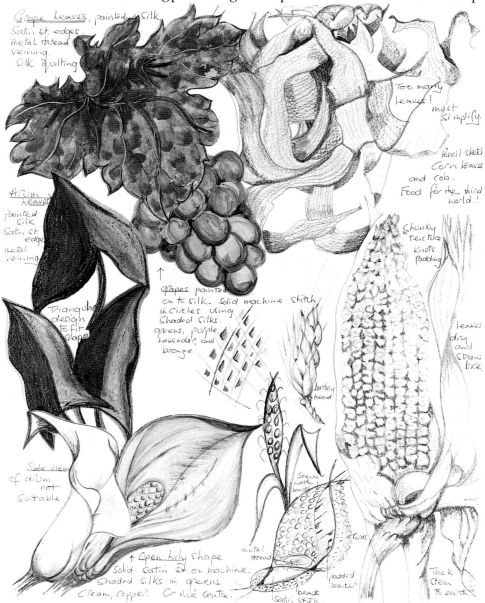

Page from Anne Raphael's sketchbook for green vestment project.

Detail from green chasuble designed and machine-embroidered by Anne Raphael for the Church of Holy Innocents, Hammersmith, London. The leaves and corn are in Madeira metal thread; the arum-lily centre and details are worked in or nué.

Designing with metallic threads

Writing about her personal approach to using metal threads, Anne Raphael says that 'spending time in our museums, galleries and churches studying designs and techniques of metal thread work is a constant source of wonder. To create a similar effect using our new materials is exciting. Long apprenticeship resulted in perfect workmanship. So too, with our machines, practice is vital. Thread colours and textures have improved and one firm alone has some sixty metallics.

'It is useful to keep notes and record needle size, thread tension, type of stitch, bobbin and spool combination, density of finished result and how, when off the frame, the fabric tension has changed. This is very important for the correct assembly and hanging of the completed vestment. Difficulties and problems are also noted.

'Machine embroidery is not a quick technique. Often the result is too delicate to be seen in a large building and must be embellished. It is easy to create small pieces that resemble *or nué* in reverse, where the colour is applied first followed by the metal, or chunky texture, using satin stitch over wide canvas, threading the holes with plate, passing, cords or ribbons. A gold fabric, resembling cloth of gold, using a dissolvable material is exciting and a wonderful choice for angels' wings or heraldic symbols. Fabric pre-painted in gold, silver, or copper then overstitched with metallic threads is rewarding. So, too, are machine-made tassels, fringes and metal cords. It is impossible to gauge how long these threads will last. Unlike the fashion industry, where garments become obsolete quite quickly, churches expect their vestments to last for ever! They must therefore be regularly inspected. Storage conditions are often poor and over-zealous sacristans have to be persuaded not to use an iron.

'Above all, I try never to lose sight of the purpose for which the work is commissioned, nor the message it is to convey.'

BRIEFING BY THE CHURCH AS A CLIENT

Being himself an artist, Canon Peter Delaney writes from personal experience and his advice will be of great help if you are undertaking a commission.

'An artist or craftsman needs to understand clearly the purpose of a commission. From the beginning it is necessary to develop a professional relationship between client and designer. Also, from the outset an on-site visit is essential, not only to ensure a meeting between the respective parties but also so that the designer can experience the ambience of the architectural setting for the proposed design.

'Texture, shape, limitations of space, natural and artificial light sources, distance from viewer and general colour sense are all essential elements in the initial briefing. In the case of hangings, static panels and altar frontals, the exact siting, precise use and setting, needs to be understood from the beginning. A key question to ask is the long-term plans of the client with regard to any future alterations, or schemes, which may affect the surroundings of the design in question. Too often subsequent alterations ruin a perfectly placed and well-designed item.

'In the case of vestments the question of function within a set space, distance from the viewer, storage of the finished items, and their use against already-existing vestments needs to be assessed.

'A good exercise is to ask for a written brief, including an idea of costing and type of materials to be used, so that from the very outset both designer and client understand the terms of the contract in hand. Especially important is an idea of how much time can be spent and a regular opportunity to visit the site and, when applicable, to review progress.

'When discussing the content of any proposed design, try to enter into a dialogue about the nature of the subject matter, whether representational art is in question or abstract symbol. Try to convince the client that it would be a good thing if you produced several draft designs before spending time on a finished portfolio.

'Above all else, be sure you fully understand the proposal in hand, and if there is any area of doubt, question the client about his brief. Together the designer and the client can then construct a profes-

sional relationship which in the end will produce a happy working situation and confidence in the finished work.'

Examples of commissioned designs

A brief can stimulate the imagination of the designer or it may impose conditions which show a lack of understanding of the way in which an artist works, making things difficult. Discussion and an exchange of ideas are essential as a preliminary and the following examples show how this has been fulfilled.

The Meeting House Chapel of Sussex University is modern, circular and built of blocks of concrete. The colour of the glass of the windows is a feature (opposite). The brief was to relate the falls, which hang on each side, to the stained-glass windows which form a curving wall of colour behind the

Dossal hanging and one of four falls that were designed and carried out in machine-embroidery by Aileen Murray for St Nicholas, Saltdean, Sussex.

The left of two falls designed and mainly machine-embroidered by Aileen Murray for the Meeting House Chapel, Sussex University.

Frontal, designed and embroidered by Sereta Thomson for St Stephen's Church, Treleigh, Redruth, Cornwall.

Wall covering for the apse of the Roman Catholic Church of St Mary, East Finchley, London. Hand-woven and quilted fabrics, metallic materials and various types of stitchery by Irene Waller.

altar. The shapes and colours of the falls are echoed in the glass. The ecumenical nature of the Meeting House is expressed in the text 'Though we are many we are one body'.

A dossal hanging and four falls in the colours for the seasons for St Nicholas, Saltdean, Sussex (p. 82), are interesting examples of a commission carried out by Aileen Murray. The brief for the hanging was 'something uplifting' and there was some disagreement concerning the inclusion of a figure, therefore she treated the risen Christ in a very abstract style. The background was built up in multicoloured fabrics, mainly India silks, and as it was about 230 x 160cm (90 x 63in), it was constructed in sections. The gold blocks for the figure were made separately. The effect of the metallic gold varies according to the light. This well-proportioned but colourless modern church was transformed by the hanging and the falls.

Sereta Thomson was commissioned to design the altar frontal for a small Cornish country church (p. 83 (bottom)). She carried it out in machine embroidery. The brief was that past and present industry in the parish was to be represented. Included with a Celtic cross are ruined tin mines and modern machinery.

When designing the banner (p. 57), Ruth Tudor's brief was to include the 'Mother and Child', the Mothers' Union logo, a coat of arms, and the arms of the See.

The briefing that Irene Waller received from the architect, Richard Hurley, for the most interesting wall covering (above) required her to create a work which 'had a presence and authority all of its own, yet which would not be too bold and forward as to dominate or overshadow the altar in front of it'. It also had to give the onlooker the feeling that it could be passed through.

LETTERING FOR CHURCH TEXTILES

by Pat Russell

The first consideration must be the purpose for which the wording is to be used. Is it to give immediate information, for example, on a banner identifying a church or group, or is it to be a decorative element of design? In the first case, the letters used should be of familiar form, possibly based on a contemporary typeface. In the second, when readability is not of paramount importance, on the orphrey of a cope for example, much more variation can be allowed and the abstract pattern made by the letters can take precedence over clarity (p. 87 (top)).

The second consideration is the overall character of the piece of work involved and this will be mainly determined by its purpose and environment. How is it to be used? Is its setting modern or ancient, simple or complex, light or dark? All of these factors will influence the choice of letterforms and their treatment. A successful design must harmonize with, rather than shout at its environment (p. 86). Also to be taken into account is the embroidery technique to be used. Will the letters be carried out in stitchery or appliqué? The latter is probably the most usual in church textiles. Stitchery will allow for more detail and delicacy of letterform, but appliqué should be kept bold and simple.

Designing lettering is difficult and holds many pitfalls for the untrained. For readable lettering, it is probably best to base the design on a standard typeface, selecting one with suitable boldness and simplicity. A browse through a catalogue of typefaces can be of help here. Some of the more suitable typefaces are illustrated opposite.

Letters with greatly contrasting thick and thin strokes are not suitable for appliqué work, although they could form a basis for embroidering lettering. Draw the required letters first (it can help to do this on graph paper), duplicating as required by photocopier, and then cut them out and arrange them in place. Remember that the spaces between the letters are just as important to your design as the letters themselves, so train yourself to see these as elements of your design too. The letters needed

ABCDEFG

Gill Sans Serif, a standard block

ABCDEFG

Othello, a rather more freely designed letter very suitable for appliqué

ABCDEFG

Optima, letters with thick and thin strokes and slight serifs

ABCDEFG

Albertus, a well-proportioned letter with a slight indication of serif

ABCDEFG

Cable Heavy, a narrower form of block letter

ABCDEFG

Futura Display, a very heavy narrow letterform

could be increased in size on a photocopier but it should be remembered that too much enlargement will result in distortion.

For more decorative purposes, letters can be designed in cut paper. For greater flexibility, cut small strips of paper, or parts of letters, rather than whole letterforms. All letters are built up from accepted arrangements of straight and curved lines;

an 'R', for instance, consists of a vertical, a diagonal and a bow. These pieces can be cut and recut, then rearranged to make letterforms and thence words until a satisfactory design emerges.

Experiment to see how you are going to make your curves, as this is always the most difficult part with cut paper. Do not forget they can be made up of straight lines instead of curves, if desirable, and watch those spaces in between! Stab-pin the pieces to hold them in position as you are designing, always working within the delineated margins of your final design. When the composition is completed, the letters are pasted down and an accurate tracing made.

In translating designs into fabrics and stitchery, colour adds yet another dimension to the work (opposite), and is an important part of the design. Rather than have one-colour lettering on a plain background, you might use various shades of the same colour for each letter, or change the background colour from space to space; or maybe some selected spaces could be highlighted with contrasting colour. For exciting results try treating both letters and spaces in between as being of equal value and varying the colour of each, be they letter or background, as you go along.

To add surface texture, couched threads or hand or machine stitchery can be used for enrichment. If letters are edged with couched braid or with satin stitching, care should be taken that this does not make the letters too heavy and distort the proportion of letterform to space. Should it be necessary to include an appreciable amount of small lettering in a piece of work, this would be best carried out by hand embroidery, basing the lettering on a lower-case typeface. You could also try using sampler-type lettering, or free machine embroidery using a cursive lettering, similar to a copperplate handwriting.

Altar frontal, designed and carried out by Pat Russell. Verses from Psalm 107 using familiar letterforms in an unconventional way. Chapel of HMS Ark Royal.

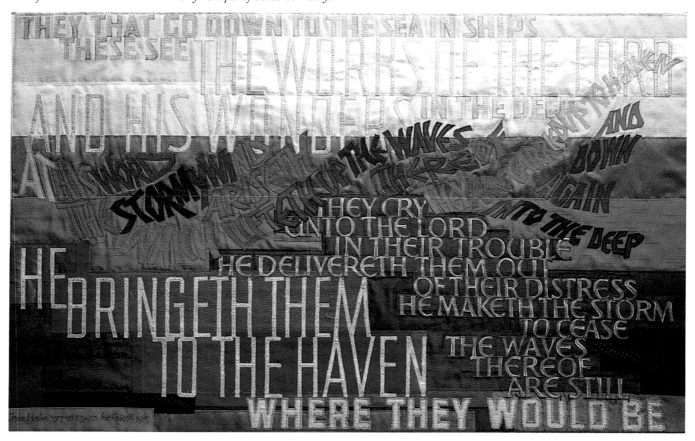

Wall hanging, designed and worked by Pat Russell.
Letters freely developed from familiar letterforms.

Banner, designed and carried out by Pat Russell. A
detail showing free machine-embroidered lettering in
St Peter ad Vincula, within the Tower of London.

CORPORATE PROJECTS

During the last century, the church gained considerably through the zeal of those women who stitched away on their huge undertakings, achieving that high standard which should never be underestimated. In this age the approach is rather different but the dedication is similar. Great importance is given to corporate projects carried out by groups of embroiderers who give their time to producing hangings, vestments, soft furnishings and kneelers for their places of worship.

Well-trained professionals and amateur needleworkers have always made an increasingly valuable contribution to the church, and with the additional instruction available today through organizations and books, also the influence of exhibitions, there should be every reason for the standard to continue to rise. The examples illustrated show how much work being created today is both original and interesting, and the techniques more inventive, together with a generally improved finish. The church benefits because stitched textiles are acquired which could not otherwise be afforded. Many a bleak interior has been improved by the introduction of an embroidery produced by a group of people who have shown the good judgement to insist upon a design of high standard.

It is not only the ecclesiastical recipients who gain; the members of the group working towards a common aim, who might otherwise be lonely, also derive immense satisfaction and pleasure from the companionship. Some of the collaborators in the project may never have taken part in the creation of a large work of art, and it is a valuable experience to witness the development of the idea.

The importance of the design cannot be over-stressed because corporate projects are generally large and will occupy a dominant position which will be a focus of interest. Designing hangings, curtains, altar frontals and copes, in particular, presents the greatest challenge and should only be undertaken by one trained to do the job – someone who has imagination and who understands the medium. The choice of designer is therefore vital, and it is essential that this experienced advice and co-operation should be sought from the beginning.

A pair of Easter banners, designed as group-work, directed by Paul Jackson and supervised by Diana Robertshaw. The project was made on a group art day. The banners were for All-Hallows-by-the-Tower, London. They hang on two pillars, north and south of the sanctuary, and relate to each other from left to right, dealing with 'Creation – From Matter to Man'.

A trained artist will recognize the general principles of design, in addition to appreciating that the character of the architecture will determine the scale. A good sense of colour will also influence the whole concept, as it will be related to the existing stained glass and furnishings, and will be changed by natural or artificial light.

The rare gift of creativity is not always appreciated or valued; indeed, sometimes technique is even rated more highly, basically because it is more easily understood. It is of primary importance to commission a good design, even if economies have to be made in other directions. A good rapport with the priest, donor and Parochial Church Council is a great help during the preliminary discussions and briefing. It is a good thing to present a choice of sketch designs, attractively mounted, with patterns of materials, together with an estimate. This is because those who are in the position to make the decisions are not always the best or more knowledgeable judges. They may be unfamiliar with an up-to-date approach or they may think in terms of words, giving them a literary interpretation, whereas the artist responds to the visual.

Ideally the designer will undertake to direct the group, as he or she will be able to help the participants understand and appreciate the inspiration behind the design. If this proves impossible, the appointment of the right person as leader of the group is important, because the wishes of the designer have to be interpreted and the workers organized. A teacher would be used to dealing with people, but she would also need to have technical knowledge and artistic appreciation. This leader would have to deal tactfully but firmly and sympathetically with the members of the group, as they will possess very mixed abilities. Most will be amateurs who are learning, and who will require time for confidence and imagination to develop. It is important that their interest is retained, and that each feels herself to be part of the creation. The leader has to keep a balance between individual initiative and the interpretation of the design.

When the piece of work is really large an important practical problem has to be decided at the outset; that is, which is the best method to select when several people are to work on the same project and there is an all-over pattern? There are several approaches, but it is the nature of the design and the technique which will determine the choice. One simple method is to divide the area into the width of the fabric, embroidering each section in a frame, by hand or machine, and taking great care to match up the pattern at the joins.

As an alternative, there are advantages in mounting the whole piece in one, large, frame: the work is kept flat, it will not pucker, and certain stitches are better worked that way. However, because it is only possible to reach about 30cm (12in) from each side of the frame, ie 60cm (24in) from both sides, that amount has to be completed and then rolled in, before another 60cm (24in) can be exposed and worked on. The disadvantage is that the participants in the embroidery have to meet and work where the frame is housed. For certain techniques the result is worth the inconvenience, especially for couched gold, long and short, laid work, appliqué and canvas work. In the same way a background (lightweight for vestments) can be framed up, and the outline of the design traced on to the fabric. Each unit of the design is planned to overlap and is completed separately, then applied. For this to be successful it has to be carefully planned.

Because a hanging is not viewed closely it can be divided up into sections for working, each person doing her own area. These are finally joined up and it is usually possible to embroider over the joins. With common sense, the position of the seams can be adapted so that they show less. A simple but rather uninteresting way to plan for several people to work together is to divide the area into decorative shapes, like patchwork on a large scale, so that each is individually embroidered and then all are joined together. In this way each piece would have been developed freehand and spontaneously.

On all corporate projects, the designer should, ideally, direct the work in an effort to keep overall unity and guide the choice of fabrics, and the value of the contribution made by the designer who assists in the realization of a project cannot be over-stressed. Thai and Indian silks are beautiful in texture and colour, but are costly, and the designer would be able to suggest a satisfactory weight in dupion, where there is a good colour range, and which is also colourfast. Artificial showy fabrics should be avoided as some colours are not fast and the colours are too harsh. If money is scarce the plainer materials are preferable.

The painted canvas, 'I came that you might have life and have it more abundantly', from St John's Gospel. Designed by Polly Hope, for St Augustine's, Scayne's Hill, Sussex.

'The Garden of Eden', designed by Polly Hope and worked by sixty parishioners for Christ Church, Spitalfields, London, in 1984. At the top of the frame are market buildings whilst down the sides are garlands of fruit and vegetables. Appliqué, machine-embroidery and quilting, 2.6m (8ft 6in) square. Also illustrated is the busy workshop for embroidering the hangings.

Alternatively, scraps and remnants can be collected together and there is always the chance of finding something beautiful or interesting.

The altar frontal (below), made under the direction of Pat Savage, the designer, demonstrates many of the points discussed. A group of people from the village of Seal in Kent wisely commissioned the design, then collected pieces of fabric, selecting appliqué and patchwork as suitable techniques. This frontal is sincere because the people concerned understood what they were doing.

The design of stitched textiles for the church has been influenced by the work of certain colleges and schools of art, and this has stimulated interest in the subject. There are groups connected to several cathedrals and churches in Britain who are engaged in creating works of real worth, inspired by their designer or group leaders. One such is the Sarum Group at Salisbury, led by Jane Lemon (pp. 14 and 44), and another is the Workshop at Derby Cathedral. The Reverend Leonard Childs' influence is far-reaching. The group from St Michael's, Highgate, London, is led and taught by Sylvia Green, who also designs the interesting and varied work which they carry out, though mainly on canvas. Currently this group is working individual buildings in Highgate Village on a project designed by Sylvia. When joined together this very large hanging is for their Parish Room.

Joan Freeman's designs are generally carried out by Clarissa Robinson (p. 19 (bottom left) and 20 (bottom)), also the York Minster Broderers. Examples of her artistry can be seen in many cathedrals and churches.

In New Zealand a group of embroiderers has created a cope and mitre of good design and beautiful colours for Dr Penny Jamieson, the first woman Bishop in the Anglican World to be in charge of her own diocese (p. 40 (top)).

Banners carried out as group projects and designed by Peter Delaney are in Southwark Cathedral and All-Hallows-by-the-Tower (pp. 88 and 89). The importance of the designer cannot be over-emphasized, and is here demonstrated by the wonderfully imaginative hanging 'The Garden of Eden', which was designed by Polly Hope and intended for Christ Church, Spitalfields, and worked by sixty parishioners (p. 91).

The painted canvas designed by Polly Hope (p. 90), is another corporate undertaking now being stitched by a group at St Augustine's, Scayne's Hill, Sussex.

Altar frontal, designed by Pat Savage and worked by members of the congregation of St Peter and St Paul's Church, Seal, Kent. Depicts contemporary village people coming anew to the welcoming risen Christ.

INDEX